RAILROADS OF NORTH AMERICA

RAILROADS OF NORTH AMERICA

EDITED AND COMPILED BY ALAN SINGER

CHARTWELL
BOOKS INC.

Edited and Compiled: Alan Singer
Copy Editor: William J. Howell
Art Editor: Deborah Miles
Design: Mark Holt

Published by Chartwell Books Inc.,
A Division of Book Sales Inc.
110 Enterprise Avenue, Secaucus,
New Jersey 07094

Set in 9/11 pt Univers Medium by South Bucks Typesetters
Limited
Printed by Fratelli Spada, Ciampino, Rome, Italy

ISBN 89009 212 5

CONTENTS

THE FIRST RAILROADS

A GREAT DIFFERENCE between Europe and North America in the 1830s had much influence over the way in which the railroads were built. In Europe, civilization had existed for centuries. Orderly communities had established a complicated structure of towns, buildings, ownership of land and rights over property, and other rights of way, including turnpike roads and canals, through which the railroads had to thread themselves. In America, a nearly virgin landscape was still being, or had only recently been, wrested from the red man, and most of the land had no individual owners at all. Turnpike roads and canals were being built, but, generally, the railroads could go where they wished without much consideration for other occupiers of the land, since there were none.

There were a few horse-tramways in of towns — though often enough the tracks were there first and the town later — and bridges rarely had to be built for them to cross roads. The tendency, especially as money was much scarcer than in Europe, was to build railways quickly and cheaply. This policy was encouraged by the government, which often granted to the companies large tracts of land in the country to be served by the new line, on condition that trains were running by a given date. The route could always be levelled, straightened, or improved by rebuilding later, and line relocations in the United States are still continuing.

There were a few horse-tramways in the Eastern States, built often to act as canal feeders; and it was on one such, the Delaware & Hudson Canal Company's line at Honesdale, Pennsylvania, that the first 'road-service' locomotive in America ran in 1829. It was the *Stourbridge Lion*, a Killingworth-type engine built in England by Foster & Rastrick of Stourbridge. Unfortunately, it was too heavy for the track and was taken out of service.

Steam locomotion really started in America on the Baltimore & Ohio Railroad, an ambitious project began in 1829. During 1831 the railroad company arranged a locomotive contest on similar lines to the one in England at Rainhill in 1829, though with even stricter weight limits, and the main part of the contest consisting of a month's practical service in traffic. Five competitors took part, all American, and the winner was a watchmaker named Phineas Davis, who entered a vertical-boiler four-wheeler. Although

WILLS's CIGARETTES.

1ST LOCOMOTIVE IN THE U.S.A.

this locomotive was not developed, it was quite a practical design up to a certain size. In fact, the last of the eighteen similar engines Davis built for the company stayed at work until 1893. By 1835 steam power had taken over from horses on the Baltimore & Ohio railroads, and many other railroads were following suit.

Left: A replica of the third steam locomotive to be built in the USA. The 'DeWitt Clinton' (constructed by the West Point Foundry of New York City; Mohawk & Hudson Railroad) made its first trial run in 1831. The similarity of the passanger cars to stagecoaches will not go unnoticed. *Cecil J. Allen Collection*

Below left: The famous 4-4-0 'General', built in 1855, earned fame on the Western & Atlantic Railroad on 12 April 1862 when it was hijacked by James J. Andrews' Yankee Raiders at Big Shanty, Georgia, and after a historic chase was recaptured by train conductor William A. Fuller. 'General' was restored to working order by the Louisville & Nashville Railroad in 1961 and is seen here celebrating the centenary of the chase at Ringgold, Gallic, Georgia, in April 1962. *Louisville & Nashville Railroad*

Right: The one-horsepower 'Tom Thumb'— America's first full-size steam locomotive, seen here in replica — built for the Baltimore & Ohio by Peter Cooper in 1830 to convince the railroad's directors that steam rail power was practicable. *Blackhawk Films*

Below: A typical 'Wild West' 4-4-0, by William A. Lendrum of Scranton, in model form. *Science Museum, London*

WILL'S CIGARETTES

LOCOMOTIVE, NEW YORK CENTRAL RLY.

Technically, the important difference between American and British railroads resulted from the former's lighter and rougher construction, and greater need to save capital outlay. British-type four-wheeled engines and carriages would not stay on the uneven rails, so they had to be provided with guiding-wheels and bogies. This in turn meant that passenger coaches, for instance, had to be built much longer, and the abandonment of compartments in favour of open saloons was then purely a matter of economics. On the other hand, the scarcity of bridges and tunnels meant that there was plenty of room to build high and wide vehicles, and the steeper gradients put early emphasis on the need to have powerful engines. American locomotive builders started by copying Stephenson's Planets and soon developed them greatly, first of all replacing the front-carrying wheels by a two-axle bogie. By the early 1840s they had evolved the standard 'Wild West' 4-4-0, a simple, robust and powerful machine which was the commonest motive-power unit on American lines until the 1880s.

As early as 1840 the Birmingham & Gloucester Railway in England, faced with the problem of working up the one in thirty-seven Lickey Incline, and hearing good reports from America, ordered fourteen typical 4-2-0s from the firm of Norris of Philadelphia. For the rest of the nineteenth century the development of railroads in the world outside Europe and America was, as a rule, in the hands of either British or American engineers and schools of design. British engineers were given a head start by their country's political dominance, but many colonial administrations found American methods better suited to local conditions.

Inset, top left: A late 19th-century 4-4-0 of the New York Central. No 999 of this class is reputed to have touched 112½mph on the newly-inaugurated 'Empire State Express' in May 1893.

Left: Another typical 19th-century 4-4-0 of the New Central, No 25 'William Mason' of the Baltimore & Ohio Railroad on display at Baltimore in 1952. *J. M. Jarvis*

Overleaf: William Norris of Philadelphia was probably the first American steam locomotive builder to win international repute. 'Austria' was one of his exports, shipped to Austria for trials in 1838, but similar Norris 4-2-0s operated on US railroads at the time. This 10-inch-gauge model was one of two built by Philip Wolfe in the early 1840s and probably used for sales promotion. *Science Museum, London*

CAMELBACKS OF THE NINETEENTH CENTURY

IN THE DAYS of steam traction, a locomotive of bizarre or unusual appearance was almost certainly influenced in its design by the need for fuel economy. Some examples near to our own time were the steam turbine locomotives of the Pennsylvania, Chesapeake & Ohio, and Norfolk & Western Railroads, which are described later in this book; the Crostis of British Railways and Italian State Railways, and the Bulleid turf-burner of Coras Iompair Eireann. None, however, became such a widespread, and effective, cult as the Wootten-firebox engines from 1877 until after the Second World War.

The exceptionally wide firebox, which usually had to go above coupled wheels, meant there was insufficient space for a cab in the normal location. So, a special cab was made to go over the boiler barrel and the driver was set to one side. The fireman was kept at the back end, so far back that he was really on the tender, and was rarely given more than the scantiest protection.

Such engines, use of which was almost wholly confined to the United States, were from early days colloquially known as camelbacks or Mother Hubbards. There were even times when they were referred to as such in the staid reports of the Interstate Commerce Commission. Mother Hubbard arose from the large windowed cupboard appearance of the wooden cab astride the boiler; camelback arose similarly from the hump-like contour of the locomotive's side elevation. The ugainly arrangement resulted from the use of anthracite fuel, and the type appeared first on those railroads which, from around 1840, had been using anthracite for their locomotives. From 1840 to 1850, the early examples had been known as camels, and were associated particularly with the builder Ross Winans. They had a fairly narrow firebox entirely behind the rear pair of wheels — a long-boiler type, in fact.

There was one big difference. The camels used top-quality anthracite and big firebox capacity was not essential for such fuel; but a larger grate than usual was desirable and that could be obtained from extra length as easily as from extra width. With a few exceptions, the long-grate type was in use until the mid-1870s on the roads that served the large anthracite beds. Winan's own engines often had fireboxes of remarkable shape,

not unlike some of Crampton's in England.

A feature of the anthracite industry was that the handling and preparation of the friable fuel resulted in an immense amount of dust (culm), reckoned at times to represent eighteen or twenty per cent of the whole production. It was gathered into enormous heaps at any convenient place near the breakers, and abandoned, for it was too fine for domestic use or general industrial purposes. To make use of the huge quantities of culm, John E. Wootten evolved his

patent firebox, for as the culm could be had almost for the asking, he foresaw a big reduction in his railroad's fuel bill if he could use it without running into consequential troubles. His success was evident in a reduction of $380,000 a year in the cost of coal to the Philadelphia & Reading road when 170 to 200 Wootten-box locomotives were in service in 1884.

A wide firebox does not make a Wootten. Ivatt's big-boilered Atlantics on the Great Northern Railway in England were often referred to as Wootten types,

but they were not. The Wootten box was an extremely wide and exceptionally shallow structure designed specifically to burn culm, or buckwheat anthracite as it was sometimes called. As such, it had a very large grate to give the low firing rate needed with dust, and the small firebox volume that is sufficient for the short flame of anthracite. To suit the thin but very hot bed of fire, the grate bars were nearly always in the form of water-tubes.

So shallow were the earlier boxes that the top of the coal bed could be level with the bottom row of tubes; and common practice was to put a low brick wall across the front of the grate so that, even with comparatively high firing rates, the dust would not be carried straight through the tubes. This arrangement, and a combustion chamber, were parts of Wootten's master patent of 1877; but a later patent provided even for boxes wherein the grate bars were a few inches *above* the bottom tubes – to suit engines with larger wheels than those of the normal freight engine of the time and yet retain a low boiler pitch.

However, such nice considerations of space were eased as soon as it was realised that a low centre of gravity to the locomotive was no longer essential, and that boiler pitch could be raised appreciably. Credit for achieving the change of design in North America is usually given to Theo N. Ely, of the Pennsylvania Railroad, in his bituminous coal-burning K-class 4-4-0s of 1844. Actually, Wootten was the first to introduce the practice when he went to 7ft 8in pitch in 1880, 2in more than Ely's figure of four years later.

This heightening of boiler pitch solved the teething troubles experienced by the Wootten boilers of 1877-79. Also it enabled a flat grate to be used instead of the slightly sloped early boxes; and the combustion chamber was shortened or almost eliminated, thereby reducing construction costs. Further, the higher pitch increased the possible application of the box to 4-4-0s, thus removing its earlier restriction in use to small-wheel freight and mineral 4-6-0s.

Absence of teething troubles on any scale was much due to the audacity with which Wootten, as general manager of the Philadelphia & Reading, tackled the business. Previously, he had for five years been superintendent of motive power of the road, and he realized fully that large grate area was essential to give the slow combustion rate needed. But not many men in a position of full responsibility

would have gone from the 18sq ft of large American-type 4-4-0s at one bound to 64sq ft, and within three years to have gone up to 76sq ft. Provision of such a grate naturally changed locomotive appearance considerably, and introduced some problems of weight distribution. In those days, the very weight of the box itself was more than could be supported on a single trailing carrying axle; but in any case such wheel arrangements had not really arrived in 1877-80, even for normal boiler locomotives.

From 1880 Wootten-box engines went straight into the main-line class; in the previous three years the twenty-five or so locomotives fitted had been slow-speed freight and mineral haulers with six-coupled wheels; and the still older camels had been mainly 0-8-0s. The Philadelphia & Reading 4-4-0s of 1880-84 were far larger than any others in the United States at that time, and had cylinders of 20 and 21in bore, usually with a short 22in stroke. They had a pressure of 140lb; a firebox heating sur-

Below: Baltimore & Ohio Railroad's jaunty-looking camelback ten-wheeler of 1873, with Winans-designed boiler and cab.
Chesapeake & Ohio/Baltimore & Ohio Railroad Co

face of 130 to 150sq ft out of an evaporative total of 1,100 to 1,200sq ft; a grate area of 65 to 76sq ft, and a weight of 47 to 50 tons. Wheels were 60 to 65in, the firebox was above them, and the enormous ashpan, with hand-operated hopper doors at the bottom, was wholly between the frames, for trible-section pans were out of the question with the revolving side rods.

Following the general practice with wood-burning American-type 4-4-0s, the blast nozzle was adjustable from the cab, and set low down in the smokebox, often level with the bottom row of tubes. Centralized coupled-axlebox lubrication from a single oilbox began with these engines. Although outside side-valves were commonly operated from inside Stephenson motion through cross-shafts, the first use of Joy radial motion in the USA was on one of these Philadelphia & Reading 4-4-0s in 1882 — and in his diary Joy recorded how the engine rocked and rolled at bad places, and what a great slam the weight of the big firebox at the back end produced when going over a soft spot at a mile a minute.

The curious position of the cab was not a feature of the earliest Woottens; in fact it had a European origin. Wootten sent a 4-6-0 to an exhibition in Paris in 1878, and at the closure one or two trial runs over the French Nord and Est systems were proposed. The loading gauge would not pass the cab as it was originally built, spread out over the firebox, in which engineer and fireman were together. Therefore a cab was fabricated in France

to go over the barrel, and the driver went with it. From 1879 Wootten adopted the same practice in America, as it solved in advance difficulties of growing boiler and firebox sizes, even within the generous American loading gauge.

Separation of the driver and fireman was not accepted readily by leading railroads, even though there was a side platform or walkway connection between the two, and sometimes a speaking tube. The Pennsylvania did try camelbacks once, on the first three Atlantics it possessed; but the idea of a separated crew was rejected within a matter of weeks, and the engines were transferred to the subsidiary Long Island Railroad. The Pennsylvania, however, was a bituminous coal road, and had no real economic use for Wootten fireboxes. The

Below: One of the solitary class of Mallet compound camelbacks, Erie Railroad 0-8-8-0 No 2600. *V. Goldberg*

Bottom: Lehigh Valley Railroad's camelback 4-4-0 No 424 'James Donnelly' heading the system's 'Black Diamond' express at Easton, Philadelphia, in May 1896 just before the train's first run. *C. T. Andrews*

Right: An extraordinary machine, one of several built by Norris of Philadelphia for the Camden & Amboy line in 1847-52 after the C & A president had taken a fancy for the European single-driving-wheel express passenger engines. The driving wheel was 8ft in diameter and the gaps between its spokes were filled with wooden insets. The six-wheel leading truck was unique to this class until 1939.

WILL'S
CIGAR

EARLY LOCO

OTIVE, U.S.A.

anthracite roads, such as the Pennsylvania & Reading, Lehigh Valley, Lackawanna, Delaware & Hudson, and Central of New Jersey, took up the idea for both freight and passenger power; but with a few exceptions their trains did not run at high speeds.

An important exception was the Camden-Atlantic City flyers of the Pennsylvania & Reading, and for those trains, Wootten-box single-drivers, 2-4-2s and then Atlantics, were developed; it was to compete with the speeds put up by the Atlantics that the Pennsylvania first turned to the 4-4-2. The Reading's (P & R's No 507) first 4-2-2 ran only trial trips in 1880, and was then taken back by Baldwin, as the Reading was in poor financial shape at the time and the builder feared for his money.

The practice of spreading the Wootten-box out over trailing carrying wheels, which were highly loaded, started with P & R's No 507. It led, also, to two further single-drivers for the P & R, rare birds for the USA, and even rarer in Britain for they were of Vauclain compound type. A few years after their construction in 1895 they were converted to two-cylinder simple-expansion 4-4-0s.

The Reading's P-class Wootten-box Atlantics, with 84in and 86in wheels, gained a reputation for speed on the Atlantic City route, running the 55½ miles non-stop at first in 60 minutes, and then to accelerated timings, until one special run was timed at 46½ minutes, or 71.6

mph start to stop. The Reading's final camelback passenger development was a 4-4-4 with a grate area of 108sq ft, but the four engines of 1914-15 were converted to 4-4-2 after a year or two.

Mother Hubbards of 4-4-0, 4-6-0 and 4-8-0 arrangement were favourites for passenger and freight traffic, and the Lehigh Valley's crack passenger train, the *Black Diamond*, ran between Jersey City and Buffalo for years behind Wootten-box 4-4-0s with 80in wheels. There were a number of three-cylinder camelbacks, a few of which had two sets of valve-gear conjugated on Gresley's system. At least sixteen different wheel arrangements were known, varying from single drivers to decapods, plus one class of three 0-8-8-0 Mallet compounds on the Erie road. Only one tank engine type was known – a 2-6-6T. About forty different railroads used camelbacks at one time or another, some of them having only a single example. About ninety-five per cent of the total number of camelbacks were on the eastern roads running through or touching the big anthracite deposits; exceptions included the Southern Pacific, Union Pacific, and Canadian Pacific, which had no more than a handful each.

Firing a camelback was a formidable process. It was undertaken more or less out in the open, on the front of a bucketing tender, with only a couple of side chains as protection against falling-off and rarely more than a curved plate above – and often not even with that. There

were two fireholes, so that fuel could be got into the back corners of a box 8ft to 9ft wide. Not often did one man have to shovel more than 3,000lb an hour, but shovelling culm was not always as easy as firing the same amount of bituminous coal; great skill was needed to keep a thin even fire free from holes over a box 8ft to 9ft wide and 9ft to 12ft long.

Culm could not be handled by the mechanical stoking devices that existed up to the early 1920s. After that, they were hardly considered, for from 1918 the Interstate Commerce Commission banned further new construction of Mother Hubbards. Separation of the crew was not favoured by unions or railroads; the driver was almost helpless if a side-rod broke at speed, so the number of camelbacks in traffic slowly decreased.

However, the last engines did not disappear from regular service until 1954, though from the end of the Second World War, when there were still over fifty in traffic, the only road operating them normally was the Central of New Jersey, which used its 4-6-0s with 90sq ft of grate area on local passenger trains until the end. One of them, No 592 built in 1901, is preserved in Baltimore; a Lackawanna 4-4-0 is on exhibition in St Louis; and a small 0-4-0, that began life on the Reading road and was subsequently in industry, is preserved on the Strasbourg Railway in Pennsylvania, though last reports are that it is no longer in working order.

ATLANTICS TO NIAGARAS THE GREAT PASSENGER LOCOMOTIVES

AT THE beginning of the twentieth century the 4-4-2, or Atlantic, dominated American Railroads, having recently superseded the 4-4-0 in order to obtain the greater boiler capacity needed to cope with increasingly heavy passenger stock. First introduced on the Atlantic Coast Line in 1894, the 4-4-2 was soon adopted by many railroads, including some in the west, but it became particularly associated with railroads serving the eastern seaboard – the Pennsylvania Railroad; the Philadelphia & Reading Central Railroad of New Jersey, and the Atlantic Coast Line itself.

Many of the early American 4-4-2s were not objects of beauty, some being of the camelback or Mother Hubbard type (described on pages 12-15) in which the fireman was banished to a vestigial cab at the rear to stoke the huge Wootten firebox. Boilers became ever bigger, and after about 1905 the driver was reunited with his fireman and the curious camelback form mercifully disappeared. Nevertheless, 4-6-0s of that pattern operated in commuter service until 1954 on the Central Railroad of New Jersey, which obtained from the Brooks Locomotive Works in 1902 three camelback Atlantics with 7ft driving wheels and 82sq ft of grate.

A large proportion of American 4-4-2s were compounds. Many of the earlier examples built in the 1890s and early 1900s operated on the Vauclain principle with high- and low-pressure (outside) cylinders one above the other, cast together in one piece, and having a common crosshead. Few if any tandem compounds were built for passenger service (as they were for freight) and during 1904-6 a number of Cole so-called balanced compounds were built, both with divided and unified cylinder drive. The same principle was applied to some early 4-6-2s, for example, on the Northern Pacific, but the advent of superheating virtually ousted compounding overnight as far as new passenger locomotive construction was concerned.

Nevertheless, the Atchison, Topeka & Santa Fe Railroad combined compounding and superheaters in 4-4-2s and 4-6-2s built as late as 1910 and 1911 respectively. Initiated in the USA by the redoubtable Cole, in 1905, the superheater was becoming well-established by about 1910. From, say, 1912, super-

heated two-cylinder simple-expansion locomotives became the almost invariable standard for new American passenger locomotive construction until the end of the steam era.

The outstanding American 4-4-2s were those of the Pennsylvania Railroad, which, almost alone in the USA, designed, developed and built its own locomotives; they were further distinguished by the Belpaire firebox. The first Pennsylvania RR 4-4-2 (Class E1) was built in 1899 and there followed from its Altoona shops several varieties, including Cole compounds. A de Glehn compound 4-4-2 was experimentally purchased from France.

Although a 4-6-2 was bought for experiment in 1907, PRR 4-4-2 development continued and in 1910 three large-boilered engines using saturated steam (Class E6) were built; they eclipsed in haulage capacity the first PRR-designed 4-6-2s built the following year which weighed twenty-two per cent more. Superheating was in vogue at that time (c 1910) and it was soon to revolutionize locomotive practice the world over. As a result, a superheater 4-4-2 (Class E6s) was built in 1914 which put out a phenomenal maximum of 2,448 indicated horsepower, making it effectively the most powerful four-coupled locomotive ever built. Eighty of the PRR E6 class were built and extensively used east of Harrisburg between New York and Phila-

delphia. All survived the Second World War, and three lasted until as recently as 1955.

The Philadelphia & Reading, no doubt inspired by the PRR's four-coupled powerpack, built 4-4-4s in 1914-15. The first American exponent of the trailing four-wheeled truck, the new P & R engines had Wootten fireboxes with grates of a monstrous 108sq ft, scarcely to be excelled even by a 4-8-4. Very unstable in operation, the rare machines were soon rebuilt as 4-4-2s and never matched their Pennsylvania counterparts.

With the appearance of the Reading 4-4-4s and the last PRR E6s in 1915, four-coupled locomotive development in the USA almost ceased – but not quite. Just twenty years later, after the economic depression of the early 1930s, a pair of gaudy orange-and-red streamlined new 4-4-2s with 300lb boiler pressure appeared on the Chicago Milwaukee & St Paul RR in 1935. They had been evolved to counter the rival Burlington Route's new high-speed diesel train and haul a lightweight luxury five-car train 400 miles in 400 minutes, with scheduled maxima of 100mph en route.

Unlike all previous American non-compound 4-4-2s, cylinder drive was on the leading coupled axle and the wheelbase was well spaced out. Oil firing imposed no limit on sustained maximum output as it did on the hand-fired Pensylvania 4-4-2. An experimental 4-4-4 also appeared on the Baltimore & Ohio Railroad at the same time and there were several smaller examples of this type on the Canadian Pacific north of the 49th parallel, but the outbreak of war a few years later made all those light four-coupled machines white elephants for the rest of their short lives.

The Pennsylvania E6s set a commendable standard with their superb boilers that could supply any amount of steam the cylinders demanded; but there was still one severe limitation – adhesion. First introduced in the United States as early as 1850, the 4-6-0 was already rapidly becoming obsolescent, except in secondary service, by the end of the nineteenth century. In a 4-6-0 it was not easily possible to combine a large wide firebox with large-diameter driving wheels.

During the early 1900s, a number of 2-6-2 tender engines, or Prairies, were built for express passenger service. Probably the outstanding examples were ten with 79in drivers built by the Brooks works (by then a part of the American Locomotive Company) in 1905 for the Lake Shore & Michigan Southern Railroad. They held the highly ephemeral distinction of being the largest passenger engines in the world until they were superseded by even larger 4-6-2s on the same railroad in 1907. A subsequent batch (1906) ranked among the earliest applications of Walschaerts valve-gear in passenger service in North America. Having an adhesive factor as high as almost 6.0, they should have been very surefooted machines. However, instability at speed because of the leading pony truck led to the rapid fall from favour

of the 2-6-2 type in high-speed service, although smaller-wheeled Prairies lasted on the Northern Pacific until the end of steam around 1958. A leading bogie was certainly necessary.

The 4-6-2, or Pacific, made its effective debut on the Missouri Pacific road in 1902 and on the Chesapeake & Ohio a few weeks later; it had become widely used and had increased dramatically in size and capacity by 1910. Large-boilered saturated-steam 4-6-2s with piston valves and Walschaerts valve-gear built by American Loco in 1907 for the New York Central and Pennsylvania Railroads (for trial) could be said to be the progenitors of the modern American steam passenger locomotive. The earliest 4-6-2s had inside Stephenson valve-gear and inboard steamchests, or even slide-valves, but external Walschaerts or Baker valve-

Left: The zenith of Atlantic design – the streamlined type built by the Milwaukee Road for its Chicago-Twin Cities 'Hiawatha' in 1934-37. These machines frequently ran at 100mph and more.

Right: A 4-8-2 Mountain type heads a one-time Cotton Belt Route passenger train out of Dallas. *Blackhawk films*

Below: One of the Pennsylvania Railroad's dependable Class K4 4-6-2s at the head of a westbound passenger train in the Pennsylvania mountains in August 1952. *J. M. Jarvis*

Overleaf: The 4-6-2 was built from 1902 to 1930 and for most of that time was America's standard high-speed passenger engine. Here, in 1952, Milwaukee Road's 4-6-2 No 157 works on an evening commuter train out of Chicago. *J. M. Jarvis*

gear and piston-valves soon became standard.

Outstanding among the almost innumerable American 4-6-2 designs was the Pennsylvania K4s first introduced in 1914, of which no fewer than 425 appeared. The K4s was essentially a six-coupled enlargement of the E6s 4-4-2 and although several were updated with roller-bearings, poppet-valves and so on, it was basically the rugged piston-valve 4-6-2 of 1914 (with the later addition of a mechanical stoker) that was still handling the backbone of the Pennsylvania passenger services thirty years later.

The K4s ran with a variety of tenders of increasing size. The original engine had a small tender with capacity for 7,000 US gallons of water and twelve and a half short tons of coal, but some later engines hauled immense sixteen-wheelers holding 24,400 gallons and twenty-five tons of fuel, such were the increasingly heavy trains headed and the longer distances

run between engine changes. An attempt to develop the K4s yet one stage further into the K5, with higher boiler pressure but retaining the same 70sq ft of handfired grate, met with little success and only two such engines, one with Caprotti poppet-valve-gear, were built.

By the time the last new 4-6-2 entered service on the Pennsylvania Railroad in 1929, a development manifested on the rival New York Central, which had itself progressively developed the 4-6-2 for over twenty years, in many respects rendered obsolete the Pacific in heavyduty passenger service. In 1927 the NYC challenged the PRR by placing in service the first of 275 4-6-4 Hudsons on its highly competitive New York-Chicago run. The trailing four-wheeled truck permitted a larger, mechanically-fired, grate and much greater power than in the handfired Pennsylvania 4-6-2.

The NYC 4-6-4s also were improved considerably during their eleven years

of construction. The last examples could develop twenty-five per cent greater maximum power for a mere five per cent more weight. The improvement was achieved mainly through incorporating a combustion chamber in the firebox and the extensive use of high-tensile nickel alloy steel in the boiler plates and running gear. The earlier engines had Walschaerts valve-gear which was later replaced by Baker gear — a peculiarly American derivative more suitable to cope with maximum valve travel lengths of the order of $8\frac{1}{2}$in. Later engines also had disc or Boxpok driving-wheel centres designed to reduce weight and inflict less wear on the track. As with the Pennsylvania 4-6-2s, the size of tenders steadily increased.

Although the best known, the New York Central Hudsons were by no means the largest American 4-6-4s. In the late 1930s, streamlined high-speed examples with 84in drivers were built for the

Left: The forlorn shell of a Milwaukee Road streamlined 4-6-4, arguably the finest express passenger design in US steam locomotive history – styling was by Otto Kuhler. No 103 was awaiting the breaker's torch at Milwaukee in the summer of 1952. *J. M. Jarvis*

Top: A New York Central Hudson 4-6-4, No 5449, still in steam at Albany, New York, in 1952. *J. M. Jarvis*

Above: A streamlined New York Central Hudson, styled by New York industrial designer Henry Dreyfuss, at the head of a typical front-rank NYC express of the 1940s. *Ian Allan Library*

Chicago, Milwaukee & St Paul and Chicago and North Western Railroads. When new, the engines regularly exceeded 100mph, and legendary tales were told of them. The heaviest and last were five built by the Baldwin Locomotive Works in 1948 for the Chesapeake & Ohio; they had sophisticated Franklin poppet-valve-gear and weighed 198 tons apiece without tender.

Many American locomotives of the early twentieth century were of decidedly austere appearance, but that was certainly not true of later machines. The visit of the British Great Western 4-6-0 *King George V* to the United States in 1927 impressed many American railroad officials and a conscious effort followed in many quarters to conceal extraneous pipework beneath boiler jackets and to improve appearance generally. Nevertheless, American engines retained a handsome, if essentially functional, appearance to the end. The huge boilers of later years left little room inside loading gauges for them to be cluttered with such protruberances as feed-waterheaters and air pumps, as had been prominent in the early 1920s.

In time, the limitations of six-coupled wheels, even when supported by adequate boiler capacity, began to make themselves felt. The 4-8-2 featured relatively little in front-rank passenger service, being more of a mixed-traffic/fast-freight type, of which the somewhat conservative New York Central and Pennsylvania Railroads operated huge fleets with driving wheels of 69in to 72in which were frequently pressed into passenger service. The Great Northern Railroad had some 4-8-2s with cylindrical Vanderbilt tenders built by Baldwin in 1923, which handled the crack GNR *Oriental Limited* for some years — there were some almost identical examples on the Canadian National road.

By the time passenger loadings generally demanded eight-coupled wheels the so-called Super Power concept, with four-wheeled trailing truck, had arrived. The result was the 4-8-4, which epitomized the final heroic period of North American steam railroading, from 1930 to 1950. A passenger 4-8-4 of 1940 represented a tremendous advance over its 4-6-2 counterpart of only twenty years earlier. It would develop about 60,000lb of tractive effort compared to 40,000lb, although the size of its cylinders could still be much the same because of a rise in boiler pressure from 200lb to 300lb per square inch. In place of the bar frames and separately cast cylinders of the 4-6-2, there was a cast single unit in the 4-8-4, which also often had the refinement of

roller-bearings in place of plain journals.

The three big American locomotive builders Alco, Baldwin and Lima all built appreciable numbers of 4-8-4s, as did several railroads in their own shops. These locomotives were all remarkably uniform in their bare essentials, having

two cylinders (except for one obscure experimental unit on the New York Central) and round-topped fireboxes, except for one series with Belpaire on the Great Northern. One of the few major variations was in valve-gear—Walschaerts or Baker, although one 4-8-4 for the NYC in 1946 was given poppet-valves. The final series of 4-8-4s on the Union Pacific were unusually equipped with double blast-pipes and double chimneys.

A few 4-8-4s were streamlined — almost entirely for publicity purposes rather than to improve performance. Among the most striking of the streamliners were the great orange-and-red oil-burners of the Southern Pacific, which hauled the SP's *Daylights* down the California coast well into the 1950s. The black bullet-nosed 4-8-4s of the Norfolk & Western with 70in drivers developed a record 80,000lb traction without booster and could exceed 100mph with ease.

The heavier American 4-8-4s represented probably the largest high-speed steam motive power on rails possible within the generous confines of the US loading gauge. The maximum diameter of boiler fixed an upper limit on steaming capacity. The largest 4-8-4s could develop 6,000-7,000 cylinder horsepower, of which 4,000-5,000hp emerged at the drawbar. The massive and robust machines were exploited ruthlessly both in power output and endurance. The oil-burning 4-8-4s of the Atchison, Topeka

Top: No 620, a Chicago & North Western Pacific streamlined in the 1940s to head the 'Minnesota 400,' leaving Chicago on an ordinary passenger train in May 1955. *V. Goldberg*

Left: Union Pacific Northern 4-8-4, built by Alco in 1944, at Cheyenne, Wyoming, in September 1969. *P. B. Whitehouse*

Below: Norfolk & Western 4-8-2 No 132, of Class K2a built by Alco in 1918-19 as a standard engine but streamlined and modernised by N & W in 1945, seen here at Roanoke, Virginia, in September 1951. *J. M. Jarvis*

& Santa Fe Railroad, the *heaviest* ever at 231 long tons without tender in the final Baldwin series of 1943-4, regularly ran right through the 1,791 miles between Kansas City and Los Angeles with six refuelling and sixteen water stops, and eleven changes of crew.

Facilities were developed to achieve long through runs with coal-burning steam power. Refuelling was carried out by overhead chutes at stops, where the ashpan was emptied and the fire cleaned. The latter-day 4-8-4s of the New York Central, delivered in 1945-46, when new regularly ran the 928 miles throughout between Harmon (thirty-three miles north of New York) and Chicago. With the provision of water pick-up apparatus, rare in the United States, the engines carried no less than forty-one long tons of coal, thus necessitating only one coaling stop on the run. Equipped with every modern device, the NYC 4-8-4s were the most intensively utilized steam locomotives ever built. When new, representatives were pitted against diesel-electrics to determine the future NYC motive power policy and covered over a quarter of a million miles apiece per annum, a truly amazing figure !

One curious departure from normal at that late stage was the short-lived Pennsylvania Duplex 4-4-4-4. Later 4-8-4s had attained such a size that they were beginning to suffer self-strangulation from their huge cylinders and limited valves, while the corresponding heavy machinery revolving and reciprocating at high speeds virtually destroyed both the locomotive and the track upon which it ran. The fifty-two Pennsylvania 4-4-4-4s were thus 4-8-4s with four small cylinders and lighter moving parts and two sets of four-coupled wheels. Excessive slipping and high maintenance costs associated with the complicated poppet-valve-gear only accelerated the influx of diesels while the engines were still new.

A modern American steam passenger locomotive of the 1940s weighed about twice as much as its counterpart of the early 1900s, but such were the technological advances made in the intervening period, particularly in superheating but also in metallurgy, that it could develop between three and four times more power. For instance, an early non-super-heated NYC 120-ton 4-6-2 of 1907 developed a maximum of 16.7 indicated horsepower per long ton (2,000ihp), which was precisely half that of the 210-ton Niagara 4-8-4 of 1945 when worked all out at 7,000ihp.

American locomotives were almost invariably worked at high power outputs, with attendant colossal firing and combustion rates. Under such conditions, boiler thermal efficiencies often sank to fifty per cent and below. Spectacular to witness and to hear in full eruption, such prodigal consumption of increasingly costly coal was a contributory factor to the rapid supersession of steam by diesel-electric in the USA in the late 1940s and early 1950s, when many still-new steam machines were consigned to the scrap-heap.

Below: No 2928, a late Northern 4-8-4, working hard on the 'California Limited' near Romero, New Mexico, in October 1947. The chimney can be extended by air-operation from the cab to deflect smoke. *R. H. Kindig*

Bottom: Pennsylvania's shark-nose Class T-1 duplex-drive 4-4-4-4 No 5537 leaving Fort Wayne with the fast mail for Chicago. *Cecil J. Allen Collection*

Overleaf: New York Central's Hudson No 5280, near the end of its career, heads the 'Empire State Express' past Dunkirk, New York, in 1952. *J. M. Jarvis*

THE GIANT ARTICULATEDS

F ROM THE FIRST 334,000lb 0-6-6-0 in 1903, Mallet articulated locomotives in the USA were 'the biggest locomotive in the world', far surpassing all Garratts, and culminating in the 772,000lb Big Boy 4-8-8-4s of the Union Pacific in 1941. That weight was for the engine alone; the combined engine and two-thirds loader tender total was just over 1,100,000lb. Several other classes in the 1930s and 1940s topped the million-pound mark with tender, but apart from the special Erie and Virginian triplex models, only three got above 700,000lb engine weight.

Among notable holders of the 'largest', meaning 'heaviest', title from 1903 were the Baltimore & Ohio 0-6-6-0 No 2400, the Erie 0-8-8-0s of 1907 (the only three Mallets with Wootten fireboxes), the first Southern Pacific oil-burning 2-8-8-2s of 1909, the Santa Fe's rebuilt 2-10-10-2s with flexible boiler joints of 1911, the Virginian 2-10-10-2s of 1918, and the Northern Pacific's Z5 class 2-8-8-4s of 1929-30 which had the largest grate area ever 182sq ft. These examples exclude the Erie triplex engines of 1913-16 and the one Virginian triplex of 1916, but all four of them were Mallet tank engines, the only standard-gauge examples in the States, though there were narrow-gauge Mallet tanks for some of the Colorado lines.

From the mid-1920s the 'largest' were no longer four-cylinder compounds but four-cylinder simple expansion; they retained the system of articulation evolved in 1884 by Anatole Mallet, whose system of compounding dated back to 1874.

Adopted first by the newly formed Alco combine after close study of the Gotthard-line 0-6-6-0s and other European Mallets of lighter weight, the Baltimore & Ohio engine was seventeen per cent heavier than the biggest rigid-framed engine of the time, and its adhesion weight was forty per cent more. For eighteen months after its completion the future of the Mallet in North America was uncertain; but the continued good behaviour of that twelve-wheeler throughout the year following its release from the St Louis Exposition of 1904 led to adoption of the form by other roads for steep-grade pusher service, and then for drag freight work.

The original 0-6-6-0 wheel notation died out after eighty had been built; the larger 0-8-8-0 went to a total of 150. In a sense, that finished the definite banking designs, though in practice engines with leading and trailing trucks often did pusher service. The front trucks gave rather easier riding at 20mph upwards; trailing trucks gave better airflow and ashpan conditions. So, extension began with 2-6-6-0s, 2-6-6-2s, 2-8-8-0s and 2-8-8-2s, all of which had appeared by 1909.

Few Mallets were ever built specifically for passenger service, perhaps only the Southern Pacific's 2-6-6-2s, soon rebuilt to 4-6-6-2, and a few rebuilds on the Santa Fe. On steep-grade sections normal Mallets were often employed on passenger trains, either as head-end power or as pushers.

Mallet construction, which from 1909-10 was extensive, was given a boost

Below: Baltimore & Ohio's 334,000lb 0-6-6-0 No 2400 – known as 'Old Maud' – of 1904 proved itself worth two 2-8-0s. *J. M. Jarvis*

Bottom: Norfolk & Western Class Y-6b Mallet compound 2-8-8-2 No 2174, one of a class built in 1948-52, at Hagerstown, Maryland, in August 1952. *J. M. Jarvis*

when the USA came into the First World War. Then the United States Railway Administration standardized further wartime construction on half-a-dozen new locomotive types, including light and heavy 2-8-8-2 Mallets that were quite a success. Later, some railroads, like the Norfolk & Western, based their own Mallets on the USRA designs, and that parentage could be traced even on the last-built N & W 2-8-8-2s of 1948-52.

Until the early 1920s, the big Mallets were limited in use by the number of freight cars not fitted with the latest pattern of MCB centre coupler, and starting at around 100,000lb pulled out too many drawbars with an unassisted Mallet at the head of the train. On the other hand, those were the days of immense coal trains requiring, perhaps, two 2-10-10-2 bankers at the rear and one 2-8-8-2 at the head to get 15,000 tons up an incline of one in fifty at around 8mph, with a total coal consumption approximating to fifteen tons an hour. Such trains commonly were of high-capacity limited-route wagons.

Nevertheless, by 1922 the locomotive itself, rather than centre couplers, was forming the limitation. The compound system applied to the long articulated layout, with the two steam circuits as part of one system, had reached its peak, in mechanical matters such as the size of the low-pressure cylinders, and in the sluggishness of steam and exhaust flows, which practically prevented top speeds above 25mph. That meant drag hauls scarcely above 14mph, and little more than half that on steep grades, even with pushers.

Compound development reached its peak in size with the ten Virginian 2-10-10-2s Nos 800-09 of 1918, which weighed 684,000lb engine only and had

the largest heating surface ever — 8,606sq ft. Even for Mallets they were pot-bellied, with a boiler barrel of 9ft 10in diameter; they were the only ten-coupled Mallets built new as such. Compound Mallets built from 1919 to 1924 were more modest and were mainly 2-8-8-2s. Only the Norfolk & Western thereafter developed the compound to get advantage from higher pressure; until 1924 few Mallets had above 210lb.

But that time higher freight train speeds were becoming essential, partly for quick delivery of perishables, but also for a straight increase in line capacity to take the growing traffic of all types. Mallets had given an increase in capacity over Mikados and 2-10-0s of earlier years, but in the early 1920s there were several instances where modern simple-expansion 2-10-2s, when fitted with boosters, increased the line capacity compared with Mallets of nearly twice the size, simply because the higher speed uphill more than counterbalanced the heavier load that could be taken by the Mallets.

The next stage came in 1924 with twenty-five Alco-built four-cylinder simple 2-8-8-2s on the Chesapeake & Ohio. General increase in boiler pressures in the States was still two or three years

Top: Heading coal empties in New River Gorge in September 1951 – a Norfolk & Western Class A 2-6-6-4 of 1949-50 design. *J. M. Jarvis*

Above: Denver & Rio Grande Western Class L-131 2-8-8-2 No. 3609 clambers up Tennessee Pass with a 71-car westbound freight in March 1940. *R. H. Kindig*

off, for the 240lb of the USRA designs had not been repeated, and the C & O machines had only 205lb. The increase in practicable speed which they brought was notable, and they could be got up to a maximum of 35mph on suitable sections, which meant that 14-15mph drag freight schedules could be accelerated to 20-22mph; yet the normal output of those engines was not more than 3,300 indicated horsepower at 20mph.

They were not the first simple-expansion Mallets, for the Pennsylvania Railroad built a fifty per cent maximum cut-off 2-8-8-0 in 1919, and that followed eight years after another solitary 2-8-8-2 in 1911. Nothing came of those two prototypes, and these apart the Pennsylvania had only a handful of compound 2-8-8-2s. The four-cylinder simple-expansion 2-8-8-2 soon spread to the Great Northern, Rio Grande, Southern and other roads, but only to a total of eighty-six,

for it was overtaken by developments that followed Lima's application of a four-wheel trailing truck to rigid-frame locomotives, so that by 1928 the Mallet also was appearing with two-axle trucks.

Strangely, almost the first application was a 'reverse order' 4-8-8-2 — the new breed of cab-in-front Southern Pacific Mallets for the Sierra section, which began after a fifteen year gap since the construction of the last compounds for the route. With that layout, the oil-burning firebox could be carried above the drivers, so the four-wheel truck was used mainly for better guiding at the leading end. As many as 195 of the 4-8-8-2 cab-in-front engines, which increased in weight from 481,000 to 658,000lb, were acquired between 1928 and 1944.

The first of the notable four-wheel trailing truck installations was to the twelve Yellowstone 2-8-8-4s of the Northern Pacific in 1929-30. To burn lignite from the railroad's own mines, a grate of 182sq ft was provided; the evaporative heating surface of 7,673sq ft was exceeded only by the old Virginian 2-10-10-2s, which had the A-type super-heater, whereas the NP engines had the E-type equipment.

In this second stage of Mallet development, the simple expansion, higher pressures, and greater attention to valves, valve motion, and boiler output increased substantially the effective speed and power compared with the best of the older compounds; moreover, slipping was considerably decreased as the back and front steam systems were separate and had no intersurges. One serious failing of the big Mallet remained; poor riding and instability. Simple-expansion engines could attain 35 to 40mph and occasionally more, but the riding then was almost dangerous and the imposed strains on the track very high. There was a consequential deleterious effect on the bar frames, despite the size to cope with axle loads of 70,000lb and piston thrusts above 130,000lb.

Integral cast frames, dating from around 1928 for large locomotives, eased the effect on frames, though not the actual stresses coming on them. The principle of the Mallet articulation was that the rear group was the fixed unit, and the whole front group pivoted about it, with the front end of the boiler resting on curved slides. Movement of the whole front group was inherently unstable, but the effects could be tolerated up to 30-35mph.

Simple-expansion Mallets had improved in that both steam and exhaust pipes attached to the rear cylinder group could be carried on the boiler and so needed no universal or flexible sliding joints; the front engine still needed such joints for live steam and exhaust.

In the early 1930s lateral-motion devices giving up to one inch each way of spring-cushioned side movement were adopted for the leading drivers on all new Mallets. More engines for fast freight also had four-wheel leading trucks with spring-controlled side movement instead of swing links. But only when precision-machined and precision-fitted flat sup-

Top: Southern Pacific's Class AC-12 simple-expansion 4-8-8-2s could be arranged cab-in-front to give the engineer maximum visibility.
Southern Pacific Transportation Company

Above, centre: One of Chesapeake & Ohio's famous Lima-built, simple-expansion articulated, Alleghenny 2-6-6-6s of 1941. *Cecil J. Allen Collection*

Above: At Cheyenne, Wyoming – one of the Union Pacific's simple-expansion 4-6-6-4s of 1936-42. *Blackhawk Films*

Right: Striking view of Norfolk & Western Y-6b 2-8-8-2 Mallet compound articulated No 2174 crossing Trace Fork Viaduct.
D. K. Johnson

ports for the front end of the boiler, and articulation joints that prevented 'rock 'n roll', were added to the Union Pacific 4-6-6-4 Challengers in 1935 did the Mallet become a safe mile-a-minute proposition, and the third and final stage of American Mallet development begin.

For sheer fast passenger and fast freight work the Challengers themselves were never surpassed, though many similar 4-6-6-4s followed on lines such as the Delaware & Hudson, Western Pacific, and Denver & Rio Grande Western, and about 215 were built altogether. The Norfolk & Western got equally satisfactory riding, high speeds, and a drawbar output up to 6,300hp, with a 2-6-6-4 layout, built by the road in 1936-50. The design was developed also into the huge 4-8-8-4s of the Union Pacific and Northern Pacific, and they also were no mean performers in speed, having been designed for a top speed of 70mph.

Transition from first to second stage in Mallet development had brought the type out of the pure pusher class and put it into the drag-freight long-haul range, and even just into the manifest freight speeds as they were in the early 1920s. In the 1930s increased speed, which had become essential, was made possible by the third stage in development – which also diminished the new construction of large rigid-frame 2-10-4s.

The great adhesion and power of third-stage Mallets could still be used in pusher service over crucial sections where the great capital investment was warranted. Several were so used to help traffic in the Second World War, including the Big Boys themselves up the thirty miles of an average one in eighty-five incline to Sherman summit, working there for a couple of hours or more at full throttle and sixty-five per cent cut-off, with speeds between 10 and 15 mph.

The Chespeake & Ohio, with an allowable axle load of 78,500lb on some routes, adopted the 2-6-6-6 layout to get a grate area of 135sq ft; but the Union Pacific and Denver & Rio Grande Western got larger grates above more heavily laden four-wheel trucks. No other six-coupled Mallet approached the C&O adhesion weight of 471,000lb except the handful built to the same design for the Virginian. The C&O machines were checked at above 7,000 drawbar horse-power.

Strangely, the last Mallets to be built in the United States for home service were compounds. The Norfolk & Western had never given up compound propulsion or the 2-8-8-2 wheel arrangement for its drag coal trains. It was the last Class I railroad to continue fully with steam traction, and built at its Roanoke shops from 1948 to 1952 a series of thirty locomotives which, though they had practic-

ally the same cylinder size and wheel diameter as the engines built in 1918-19, had 300lb boiler pressure, sixteen per cent greater weight, and advanced valve motion. The 39in low-pressure cylinders were notable in having 18in piston valves, probably the largest diameter ever put into a steam locomotive.

The last batch of engines brought the N&W total of 2-8-8-2s to 220. The company's charged price of $260,000 per engine and tender (2.65 times the cost of the first 2-8-8-2s in 1919) was cheap at a time when Lima was getting from the Louisville & Nashville Railroad $255,000 for a 2-8-4 roller-bearing engine and tender.

The largest steam locomotives ever were the Big Boys; built in two batches, in 1941 and 1944. The latter weighed 772,000lb and had a fourteen-wheel tender weighing 437,000lb fully laden to give a total of 1,209,000lb. With a total

wheelbase of 117ft 7in and an overall length of 127ft, they were given 135ft turntables at the principal points. The pressure of 300lb was the highest ever used in a simple-expansion Mallet, but as the cylinders were only 23¾in bore the piston thrust did not rise above 133,00lb – a long way off the maximum of 219,000lb in a rigid-frame locomotive. Next heaviest engine was the Chesapeake & Ohio 2-6-6-6 at 724,500lb, and then came the Northern Pacific Class Z5 2-8-8-4 at 623,500lb. Big Boys and Challengers also had the biggest tenders among Mallets, with 21,000 imperial gallons of water and twenty-five long tons of coal.

In forty-nine years from 1903 about 3,100 standard-gauge Mallets in twenty-one different wheel arrangements were built in the States for home service, plus the two types of triplex engines, and a few Mallet tank and tender engines of 3ft gauge for the Uintah Railway and some

logging roads. Just over forty per cent of all engines were 2-6-6-2s. Of the standard-gauge engines nearly 2,400 were compounds. So, while the later simple-expansion engines made a tremendous difference to fast freight working on a few important railroads, they by no means changed the general picture of main-line freight working throughout the United States.

THE GEARED SHAYS

AT THE TURN OF the century the West Virginian farming country at the foot of Back Allegheny mountain was as quiet and peaceful as it had been for generations; but change was coming fast, and it came in the shape of the Chesapeake & Ohio Railroad. The treasure that attracted the railway was timber and the entire Greenbier watershed was clothed in it — billions of cubic feet of some of the finest timber in America, both hard and soft. The small town of Cass grew round the railhead, and soon crews of imported Italian labourers began to lay the road up the sides of the Cheat mountain. From the summit, lines snaked away into the woods of the Cheat and Elk rivers; tracks were rough and often only temporary, and many were so crude that it seemed impossible for a steam engine to operate over them.

But the tough, geared engine, conceived by the Michigan inventor Ephraim Shay, was a match for any lumber road. Unlike the conventional steam locomotive, the Shay and its tender had all their wheels as driving wheels. All the wheels were coupled, through gears and shafts: as none could slip unless they all slipped, they gave the locomotive maximum traction. Vertical cylinders and pistons had connecting rods coupled to a horizontal

Virginia to buy the remaining engines, track and rolling stock, and convert the railway into the tourist attraction it now is. In June 1963 the Cass Scenic Railroad made its first public run. Today tens of thousands of tourists travel hundreds of miles to ride with the Shays and their half-sister, a Heisler, to the top of Bald Knob — a rail trip of twenty-two miles through the forests taking four and a half hours. The whole town has come to life again, and a piece of yesterday has been kept alive for today. More unusual for America, perhaps, it was the State which saved the day and the lame duck has not only survived but is prospering.

crankshaft that drove a reduction gear to give several power strokes per revolution of the driving wheels. As with the low gears of a motor vehicle, this provided greater ability to deal with steep gradients and heavy loads than was obtained from conventional direct coupling. The Shay engine had such high tractive efficiency that if an engine came off the road, the crew put down re-railers and it would pull itself on again.

The Spruce Lumber Company owned and worked the whole operation, from cutting and transporting timber to milling and preparing it in its final form of planks and boards. The railway also was self-contained, with its own workshops fully capable of repairing the Shays (all twelve of them) no matter what the damage. It even had its own foundry, with more than twelve hundred patterns for parts, and an engine could almost have been built from scratch there.

But within fifty years, in 1942, modern technology put an end to the big mills, and lorries overthrew the Shays. A large part of the timber country passed into the hands of the Federal Government, and the holdings dwindled to about 65,000 acres on the southern end of Cheat mountain. For eighteen years operations were continued there on a reduced scale, but from the morning of 1 July 1960 work ceased.

However, a railway enthusiast, Russell Baum, persuaded the State of West

Left: Climax-geared locomotive No 9 of the Hillcrest Lumber Company, now on display at the Forest Museum on Vancouver Island, British Columbia. *V. Goldberg*

Above: A Shay-geared locomotive of the Union Pacific, used in the Tintic mining areas of Utah, in 1940. *R. H. Kindig*

Overleaf: Formerly owned by the Spruce Lumber Company, a Shay-geared locomotive now operated by the Cass Scenic Railroad in West Virginia. *P. B. Whitehouse*

DAY CARS, PULLMANS AND DOMES: THE DEVELOPMENT OF PASSENGER CARS

THE EARLIEST carriages on rails were no more than developments of the highway coach — primitive four-wheelers — run on track which was often cheaply built and of light construction. The design soon moved to a longer vehicle on two four-wheeled trucks, or bogies, which rode very much more easily. The adoption of an open (or saloon) interior, with seats on each side of a central longitudinal aisle, has been ascribed to the 'democratic' nature of American society.

As the American railroad network grew, journeys of twenty-four hours or more became commonplace (speeds were not high) and the need arose for vehicles that were suitable for both day and night travel. Economy required that such a vehicle should be convertible and from a number of early designs George Mortimer's Pullman became most widely adopted. In the Pullman layout, groups of four seats (two facing pairs) on each side of the aisle could, by rearrangement of the cushions and backs, be made into a bed, or lower berth. An upper berth was built into the upper wall and ceiling panelling and could be lowered when required. Privacy was achieved by heavy curtains and toilet facilities were pro-vided at the ends of the cars.

American railways, with little traffic in the early days, had to be cheaply built and high-level station platforms, were an expensive luxury for only two or three trains a day. Passenger cars were built with open vestibules at each end and with steps down almost to rail level. The final gap to the ground was bridged by a portable stepping stool, placed in position during stops by a trainman.

Heating was by stove, one or sometimes two to a car, using wood, coal or occasionally oil as a fuel. Lighting developed from oil, through gas to electricity. Seats in ordinary coaches were often reversible ('walkover') and plush finished, although rattan cane was sometimes used for shorter journeys. Windows generally were narrow and could be opened upwards, to admit (in summer) a cooling draught — and dust and cinders! Sometimes, a gauze sash was fitted in an attempt to reduce inblown rubbish, and in the northerly areas, a second glazed window, or storm sash, could be fitted in winter. The adoption of the clerestory roof, which contributed both to ventilation and to lighting, was early and wide-spread, and continued to feature in new construction up to about 1930.

At first, car bodies were mainly made of wood, but increasing size of vehicles and emphasis on greater safety led first, in the latter part of the nineteenth century, to the steel underframe and eventually early in the twentieth century, to the all-steel car.

As car design developed, to meet the needs of an expanding, prosperous nation, details improved. The open-end platform gave way first to narrow enclosed vestibules, and later to full-width vestibules. Even in later years, with the very few high-level station platforms, it was necessary to provide specially for access from rail level. Doors were invariably at car ends and, outside the trucks, opened inwards. Often they were split, Dutch style, and a hinged flap with handrail on its underside lifted to reveal the steps.

A feature of American rail travel conspicuous to European eyes is the door-opening ceremony performed by trainmen, who also assist passengers joining or alighting from trains. Both halves of the

Below: Artist's impression of 'City of New York,' an early Pullman sleeper.
Illustrated London News, 10 October 1869

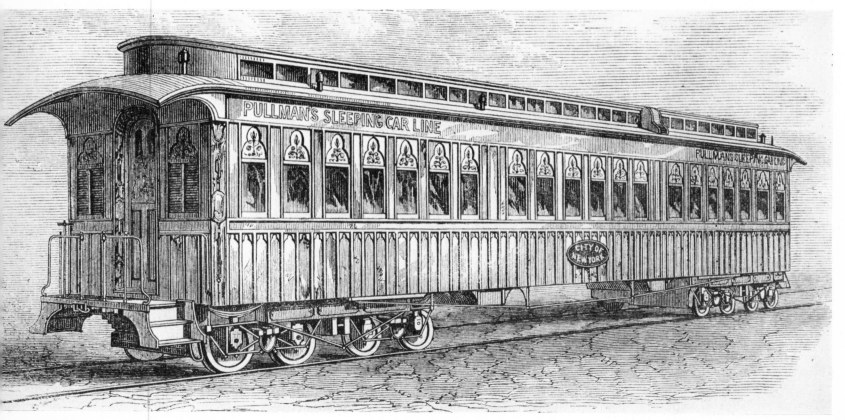

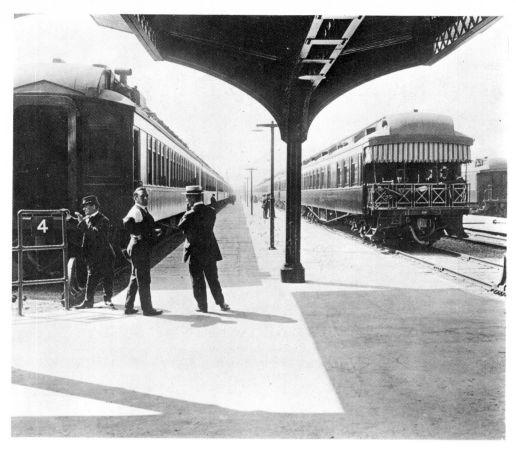

door are swung inwards while the train is slowing, the trap is lifted and clipped up, the handrail is wiped clean of dust with a paper towel after the trainman has descended to the bottom step, with the stepping stool ready, and finally, as the train stops, the stool is placed on the ground beside the steps.

Towards the end of the nineteenth century, a considerable degree of comfort was provided. Dining-cars had replaced stops for meals, so reducing journey time, and, in keeping with the times, both dining-cars and sleeping-cars were ornately decorated in woodwork of various styles in which a high level of craftsmanship was evident. Electric light was coming into use, and the Westinghouse airbrake, adopted earlier, improved not only safety but comfort in stopping. Car lengths had increased from the early 50 or 60ft to 70 or 75ft. The larger and heavier cars often rode on two six-wheeled bogies, which became universal for Pullman's sleepers and dining-cars.

The ornate finish was not confined to interiors. Externally, dark green was, perhaps, the most common livery, and 'Tuscan' red was used by a number of companies, including, up to the last few years, the Pennsylvania, and Canadian Pacific. The railway's name appeared along the 'letter board' above the windows, commonly in gold leaf, and usually in an extended Roman script with serifs. Car sides before all-steel bodies were often matchboarded and could be elaborately lined out, though that became a casualty of the First World War.

In the larger cars, windows of passenger spaces were often arched, with the upper part in stained glass. An essential feature of all American passenger cars (in contrast with British practice) was the handbrake. On open-platform cars, it was applied by a horizontal wheel but, later, vertical wheels or levers with ratchets were provided inside the vestibule. Even after automatic brakes became universal, the handbrake was, and still is, required for parking. Another universal feature from quite early days was the provision of drinking water, sometimes iced in summer, in all passenger cars.

Two classes of travel were generally provided, 'coach', that is day-coach, with sitting accommodation for day (and night) use. First class carried a different connotation from the European meaning. A first-class ticket entitled the passenger to occupy Pullman car sleeping space,

Top: The typical open-veranda observation car of the early 20th century on the right is operated by Canadian Pacific.
Cecil J. Allen Collection

Above, centre: Traditional clerestory roof in a narrow-gauge version of the Denver & Rio Grande Western at Silverton, Colorado in July, 1970. *V. Goldberg*

Left: Vista-dome car of the Norfolk & Western's 'City of St Louis' train in August 1961. *J. K. Hayward*

which had to be paid for additionally, but there was no ordinary first-class accommodation. First-class day travel could be either in a Parlor car, where a seat supplement was payable, or by day occupancy (if the train times and journey permitted) of sleeping-car space. 'Pullman' and 'sleeper' are almost synonymous in American practice.

The Parlor car, provided where daytime demand for first-class travel warranted it, was arranged with single armchairs each side of a central longitudinal aisle; it carried a Pullman porter to serve light refreshments from a pantry or small buffet. Each sleeping-car had its own attendant, or porter, traditionally a negro, who stayed with the car for each journey. He would sleep in an unoccupied berth when available; otherwise he made do in his cubicle seat, or in the smoking-room at the car end.

In the early 1900s there came the development of the all-steel car. Initially, the later ornate styles of the wooden car were continued. After the First World War (during which American railways were placed under government control), designs were much simplified; while there was no diminution in comfort, ornate decoration was largely cast aside. In its place came simplicity and standardization.

Few American railroads had or have sufficient workshop capacity to build all their own rolling stock (or, for that matter, locomotives). There is a very sizeable industry in the United States manufacturing both freight and passenger vehicles and while some railroads' railway works ('backshops') could, and did, manufacture locomotives or cars (the Pennsylvania built both at its Altoona shops), outside purchase was more common.

Interworking in traffic had long made some degree of standardization essential, and purchasing from common equipment manufacturers carried the process considerably farther, so that the 1920s became known as the Standard Era.

The use of Pullman cars was particularly influential, for the Pullman Company provided sleeping-car service under contract to almost every road which required it. The Pullman fleet rose to almost 10,000 cars by 1931, and 4,000 of them were of one basic design known as the 12-1 type. It contained twelve sections, each with lower and upper berths, plus a drawing-room for three persons with its own toilet cubicle.

For the twenty-four possible occupants of the sections, separate men's ('smoking') and women's ('rest') rooms were provided at opposite ends of the car. Each washroom contained two or three wash-basins, a dental bowl, a sofa or

Below: Canadian Pacific observation car of the first quarter of this century, with visible through the rear windows the wholly open viewing car that was added through the Rockies in the summer. *Cecil J. Allen Collection*

Bottom: Old-time clerestory-roofed stock on the preserved Silverton narrow-gauge line in Colorado, August 1966. *C. J. Gammell*

lounge chairs for three, and a single WC annexe. Towards the end of a night's journey, these facilities sometimes became heavily taxed.

The day-coach, too, might have smoking and rest-room facilities at each end, but the interior was changed only in details of the fittings; seats were still arranged in pairs on each side of the central aisle. Whereas Pullman sleepers had for years been a product of the Pullman-Standard Manufacturing Company, there were other manufacturers of coach and other passenger vehicles. American Car & Foundry was one such, with several plants, including some taken over from previously independent firms. The

heavy steel 'Standard' cars weighed eighty tons, or more, and largely rode on six-wheeled trucks. A solid train of such vehicles was an impressive sight, and no mean load for the motive power — then steam, except for a few electrified sections of line.

It is worth looking at the make-up ('consist') of a typical train of the Standard Era. Behind the locomotive came the head-end cars. Leading them would probably be a Railway Post Office car (RPO) carrying mail and with sorting facilities for en route dropping and collection. Behind the RPO would be baggage and express cars, for passengers' luggage and parcel traffic, Baggagemen,

express messengers, and postal clerks — the latter two categories often armed with revolvers — had their duties 'up front'.

Next came the coaches; often one would be set aside for local passengers making short journeys, while passengers for major stations might be directed to particular coaches, thus making on-train ticket checking somewhat easier. Between the coaches and the Pullmans came the dining-car, with its kitchen section to the rear (so that the train's draught did not blow the heat from the kitchen down onto the diners). Then came the Pullmans and, at the rear of any train worth its salt in the nineteen-twenties, an observation car, at one time with the traditional open rear-end platform and brass railings, but later more likely a solarium or enclosed lounge with large windows. Although Pullmans were convertible for day use, passengers could also sit in the lounge and, except during the period of Prohibition, enjoy a drink. The lounge-car might also have certain other on-train facilities, maybe a library, or a barber's shop with shower, or even a radio.

A long-distance through train of the period might run over the tracks of two or three companies, each of which contributed cars for the train in proportion to their part of the mileage. Often, in such cases, the regular cars for the train would carry the name of the train on the letter board instead of the company owning the car. With many journeys taking more than twenty-four hours, several sets of trains were often needed to meet the requirements of a particular service in each direction. Such, then, was railway travel in the Standard Era.

The spread of paved roads and use of private motor cars, the practical development of commercial flying and the depression made heavy inroads from 1930 into rail passenger business. Contraction was severe, but several developments in the early 1930s brought the internal combustion engine to main-line passenger service, in conjunction with new lightweight high-speed motorized trains, albeit of rather limited capacity. The Budd Company of Philadelphia pioneered the production of a much lighter type of locomotive-hauled passenger car. It had load-bearing sides of welded corrugated stainless steel. The riveted sides and clerestory roof were replaced by a sleek bright car, 85ft long, with large 'picture' windows, riding on two four-wheeled

Top: A Canadian Pacific diner of the 1920s. *Cecil J. Allen Collection*

Left: Observation car of the Southern Pacific 'Daylight' streamliner at San Francisco in 1952. *J. M. Jarvis*

trucks. The weight came down to around sixty tons, despite the fitting of air-conditioning, reclining seats, electric ice-water coolers and so on.

Air-conditioning was also applied, in the nineteen-thirties, to existing Standard cars, firstly to diners, then to sleepers, and to a limited extent to coaches. The financial position of many railways after the depression restricted investment in new stock, and led to the refurbishing of older cars, which had then to meet the enormous flood of wartime traffic, without replacement while builders were on war production work.

After the war, large orders were placed for passenger cars and in the period from about 1946 to 1957, the principal trains, and many others, on the majority of railroads were re-equipped with entirely new sets of cars. Some lines favoured stainless-steel finish, others adopted smooth-sided lightweight cars, with distinctive colour schemes. To re-equip a transcontinental train running from Chicago to the Pacific coast might require five or six train-sets with up to eighteen vehicles in each; an expensive investment.

The Pullman car changed greatly in the streamline era when there was a demand for accommodation with more privacy. The 'roomette', with a fold-away bed — a single room with built-in toilet facilities — became popular. Bedrooms and compartments each provided space for two, and drawing-rooms for three people. All except roomettes could be obtained *en suite,* for family use by folding away the common dividing partition.

Each of the vehicle types mentioned earlier was built in streamline form, although the observation car took on a round-ended rear lounge. The most distinctive post-war innovation was the dome-car. Used mainly in the west, where clearances were adequate, the Vista-dome provided glazing not only at each side, but ahead, to the rear and in the roof. It was an instant success on scenic routes. Generally, a dome was associated with a coach (second-class) configuration, with generously spaced reclining seats at normal floor level and

washrooms located beneath the dome. Dome sleepers, and dome-café cars were also built. Amtrak, the US Government corporation which now operates most long-distance passenger trains, took over the best of the streamliner equipment and still operates domes on many of its services, except in the east where clearances are tighter. But the cars are becoming fault-prone with age and, as described in a later chapter, they are being replaced by Amtrak's own new equipment.

Top: The Pleasure Dome car of Santa Fe's 'Super Chief' featured individual rotating seats in the Vista-dome observation lounge and the Turquoise Room diner below amid ships.
Aitchison, Topeka & Santa Fe Railway

Above, centre: The New Haven's New York-Boston 'Bay State Limited' near New York 149th Street station in July 1961.
W. E. Zullig Jnr

Above: 'Loch Katrine,' a Northern Pacific 'Slumbercoach' with a duplex arrangement of roomettes, at Mandan in July 1970.
V. Goldberg

THE DIESELS TAKE OVER

IF THE INTERNAL combustion engine had already been perfected by the beginning of the nineteenth century, would anyone have bothered to invent the steam engine? Almost certainly not. Once diesel engine technology had matured and its rail traction power and economy had been demonstrated in the 1930s, the only railroads to hesitate about discarding steam power were those with big commercial interests in the coal industry.

Within a dozen years the North American steam locomotive fleet was practically eliminated. In 1946 the 37,500 steam engines of the Class I railroads were still handling eighty-eight per cent of their owners' freight and seventy-

eight per cent of their passenger business. At that time just over 4,400 diesel traction units were in service. By 1958 the diesel stud had grown to over 27,600 units, which had assumed more than ninety-one per cent of passenger and over eighty-eight per cent of all freight haulage. Steam power had shrunk to a mere 1,700 engines that were mainly concentrated on ten systems. Only the Norfolk & Western was still heavily committed to steam power, constrained by dependence on coal for seventy-five per cent of its freight tonnage; but the N & W did not avoid the overwhelming trend for long.

Even electric traction succumbed. Rail electrification in North America had

never been pursued with the enthusiasm that it had enjoyed in Europe. Not only were the few projects in the United States for extension of catenary now pigeon-holed, some existing electrification came to be seen as a handicap to long-distance through working of diesel locomotives and, after the Second World War, was actually ripped out — for example, at Baltimore, Cleveland, and on parts of the Great Northern and Milwaukee roads.

The internal combustion engine had come into use on railroads early in the

Below: An EMD F7 diesel of Santa Fe heads the railroad's 'Texas Chief' at Oklahoma City. *C. V. Ehrke*

twentieth century. At first it was powered by gas. Following the pioneering construction in 1906 by General Electric for the Delaware & Hudson Railroad of a 200hp gas-electric railcar (that is, one with electric traction motors fed from a gas-engine-driven generator) over 700 such vehicles were operating on North American lines between the wars. Most of these so-called 'doodlebugs' were turned out in the 1920s. Provided they were in good order they covered light-traffic services more cheaply than steam trains, but they were too often incapacitated by faults, and they were fire-prone. They were operationally inflexible, too; no more than one other vehicle could be connected to their couplers to meet exceptional demand, or to move freight simultaneously as a mixed train – they had insufficient power.

During the 1920s the diesel-electric locomotive first appeared as a modestly-powered switcher. But the early diesel engines were too heavy and cumbersome to be an attractive proposition. By 1930 only about two hundred had been bought, and they were mostly for places where steam was discouraged as a fire hazard or an environmental nuisance. The first diesel locomotives were also handicapped by a poor power-weight ratio: Canadian National's articulated diesel-electric twin-unit No 9000 of 1928, for example, operated at a total of 334 tons weight for an output of only 2,660hp from its two Beardmore V12 engines.

An important development in rail traction came in the early 1930s when the successful compact, high-rpm diesel engine coincided with streamlined styling. The leading pioneer on the traction side was General Motors' Electromotive Division. By determined research and development it produced the 201A engine which, by marrying welded construction to new alloy steels and a two-cycle design, dramatically improved the diesel engine weight-power ratio from about 80lb to a mere 20lb for each horsepower. The Burlington road was persuaded to instal this power plant in its new lightweight three-car Zephyr streamliner that was under construction by Budd.

In little more than a month from delivery, the *Pioneer Zephyr* was despatched on an endurance test of 1,015 miles from Denver to the heart of the Century of Progress Exposition in Chicago. That run, on 26 May 1934, is now a landmark in world rail history, for the Zephyr hit the headlines by covering the whole distance in one non-stop, dawn-to-dusk journey at an untroubled average speed of 77.6 mph. The diesel engine had established itself on the railroad.

The next requirement was to adapt the new power to all rail haulage needs, not only to self-contained high-speed passenger units. In 1935 the Electromotive Division of General Motors launched a twin-unit locomotive prototype, which embodied two twelve-cyclinder versions of the 201A engine to produce a 3,600hp output for a total weight of 240 tons. Demonstrations proved that such a machine could move the same load as a

standard North American express passenger steam locomotive at half the cost in fuel per mile, certainly at a lower servicing cost and probably at reduced repair costs as well.

That same year the Electromotive Division of General Motors registered its first diesel locomotive sales, to Baltimore & Ohio and Santa Fe Railroads. In 1936, Santa Fe's two engines were heading the road's new once-weekly *Super-Chief*, hauling a make-up of Pullmans and orthodox sleepers unchanged throughout the 2,227 miles from Chicago to Los Angeles in a strikingly shortened schedule of 39¾ hours.

Most railroads which set out to buy the early streamlined diesel passenger trainsets wanted them built to their own specifications in shape, style and fittings.

Electromotive soon saw that this one-off treatment could consume the economical advantages of the diesel locomotive. Insistence on the utmost standardization in everything but livery was decisive, not merely in speeding domestic dieselization but in winning for the USA a head start in the world's diesel locomotive market which has never been surrendered. Foreign buyers soon appreciated the economy and reliability guaranteed by a line of standard models which would need little more than track or loading gauge modification to adapt to the characteristics of their own road.

The Electromotive Division started its campaign with the E-range of passenger units launched in 1938. The Es introduced the rounded-nose, set-back-cab outline that was the hallmark of the first

end of 1963 Electromotive built nearly 1,300 of this class and its subsequent refinements. In the late 1970s Amtrak still deployed many E8s and E9s, often comprehensively rebuilt, on its passenger services.

At first, the diesel was accepted as a purely passenger locomotive. As railroads discovered how easily cab and booster units could be arranged into multiple-units driven from the leading unit to add power to even the heaviest passenger trains, doubts whether they would match the mammoth steam articulateds used on mile-long freight trains began to disappear. By 1939, Electromotive was able to dispel all opposition with the 1,350hp V16 engine in the 567 series and a four-unit, two-cab and two-booster locomotive in which to show its

By the outbreak of war in 1939 the American Locomotive Co (ALCO) had turned from switcher construction to diesel locomotives to produce its 2,000hp DL-109 of 1940. Fairbanks Morse was ready to try its hand with its new opposed-piston two-cycle engine; and Baldwin (after the war to become Baldwin-Lima-Hamilton through merger) also kept an eye on the expanding diesel-unit market. But, after Pearl Harbor the War Production Board took control of both manufacture and distribution of diesel locomotives. It concentrated construction of road locomotives on the established Electromotive plant and limited everyone else to switcher building. That strengthened Electromotive's standing in the industry and gave it a supremacy which it has never lost. In fact, Baldwin-

generation of American diesels. Unashamedly, the engines were designed firstly to give the crew protection in collisions and only after that was any attention given to aesthetic effect. The first Es, both cabbed and cabless booster versions, were 1,800hp, twin-engine models. The Santa Fe and Baltimore & Ohio Railroads took most of them, and one lasted long enough to pass into Amtrak ownership.

The real success of the series was the E6 of 1938, which Electromotive had evolved with two of the new 567 series 1,000hp V12 engines especially for mass use. That engine was to be the heart of Electromotive's diesel technology for years to come, and the E6 triumphed as the world's first mass-produced, standard diesel locomotive. From late 1938 to the

potential as a 5,400hp freight hauler. Unlike the Es, which had been mounted on three-axle bogies with two axles on each bogie powered, the units in this FT locomotive were carried on two-axle bogies with all axles motored.

In a year of demonstrations on twenty railroads, at altitudes from sea-level to above 10,000 feet and in temperatures from forty degrees below to an extreme of 110 degrees plus, the FT covered more than 83,750 miles with loads up to as much as 5,700 tons and without a single failure in traffic. More than half the railroads which had tested the demonstrator promptly ordered FTs of their own. In all, nearly 7,000 units in the FT and subsequent F series, incorporating later marks of the 567 engine, had been sold to American railroads by early 1957.

Lima-Hamilton withdrew in 1956; Fairbanks-Morse retreated in 1963, and ALCO gave up building new locomotives in 1969.

Today, Electromotive is seriously challenged only by General Electric, which has been a major supplier of electric traction motors since the 'doodlebug' era. General Electric advanced from independent switcher locomotive building in the 1930s to a post-war marketing partnership with ALCO to promote road diesels under a joint ALCO-GE brand name. That ended in 1953. Seven years later General Electric decided to continue alone with its own range of road switchers, starting with the 2,500hp U25B. That proved so successful that within three years General Electric had supplanted its former partner ALCO in the industry's second place.

The road switcher was the second phase of North American railroad dieselization. The streamlined, full-bodied locomotive looked pleasing, but the more the diesel showed its versatility, the more the streamlined, single-cab showed its weaknesses. Unless two cab units were operated in multiple back-to-back, a streamlined unit had to be turned at terminals, rearward visibility not being good enough for operation with the cab at the rear. Another disadvantage was that the full-width car-body made the machinery inaccessible. Most of all, however, by the mid-1940s it was clear that any one diesel traction unit could efficiently cover a large range of assignments, from switching to road haulage.

The development that followed was the 'hood unit', in which appearance was disregarded in favour of functional efficiency. The driving-cab, set some way in along the frame, was the only full-width component of the bodywork. The casing of the machinery compartments was pinched into a thin box shape to open up a good view fore and aft from the driving-cab and to leave room for a running-plate walkway all round the locomotive. The fashion was set by Electromotive's 1,500hp GP7 of late 1949, which sold more than 2,600 in less than five years. Some 3,500 of the subsequent 1,750hp GP9 locomotive were sold for Electromotive between 1954 and 1959.

The all-round potential of the new design earned it the description of road switcher. From the 1950s, until the coming of Amtrak, road switchers all but

monopolized the assembly lines of American road locomotive manufacturers in all power ranges, from 1,500 up to a massive 6,600hp.

The 6,600hp road switcher marked the peak in high-powered locomotives. In 1963-65 both Electromotive and ALCO had built 5,000hp units for Union Pacific and Southern Pacific (ALCO's contribution was only three units, and they had only ten years' service). These units were essentially the combination on one frame of the sixteen-cylinder engine-transmission assemblies of two smaller, orthodox

road switchers in each manufacturer's range. In the Electromotive design the unit was mounted on two four-axle bogies; the ALCO model was on four two-axle bogies: all axles were powered in both types. Then, to mark the centenary of the famous Golden Spike completion of the road at Promontory, Utah, Union Pacific in 1969 ordered from Electromotive the 6,600hp DDA40X. It immediately became known as the Centennial, and forty-seven were built in the following two years.

By this time, the railroads were caught in an inflationary recession. While traffic fell, railroad managements despondently regarded the mounting costs of maintaining services. The more the power of a diesel engine was increased, the more delicate the engine became and the more frequently it required expensive repair. The loss of one 4,000hp-plus unit to workshops was much more costly than the removal from service of a 2,000hp unit. A fleet of smaller locomotives that could be formed into blocks of 6,000hp when traffic demanded seemed to be far more sensible economically. A further

deterrent to the development of ultra-powerful diesels at the time was the renewed interest by Western railroads in electrification.

By the late 1970s the market had generally agreed on 3,000hp as the sensible maximum unit. This was represented by Electromotive's SD40 range and by General Electric's best-selling range of U30 road switchers. Both have 3,600hp derivatives — the Electromotive SD45 with a V20 engine, and General Electric's U36 with a sixteen-cylinder engine — but only Southern Pacific and Santa Fe Railroads buy any quantity.

Both Electromotive and General Electric types have been used in full-width cab and car-body versions by Amtrak, and bear the designation SPD40F and P30CH respectively. The SPD40F soon showed a disastrous propensity to spread the rails on curves. After the reason was found to be the incompatibility between deteriorating track and the SPD40F's three-axle bogies and speed, several railroads imposed severe restrictions on the locomotives. The result was that Amtrak embarked on a very costly rebuilding of the SPD40Fs as shorter, two-axle bogie units like the F40PH which was subsequently procured from Electromotive.

Throughout the United States, however, the biggest-selling road switcher in the late 1970s was Electromotive's 2,000hp unit, the GP38. It figures in the traction fleets of at least half of the Class 1 railroads in the country.

On one issue, the two leading countries in the diesel rail traction industry, Germany and the United States, have never agreed. The Germans have always adhered to hydraulic torque converter power transmission systems from engine to wheels, the Americans to electric. In the 1960s, the two systems were put to comparative proof in the United States. The German manufacturers Krauss Maffei sent twenty-one twin-engined 4,000hp diesel-hydraulics for experimental service in American conditions to the Denver & Rio Grande Western and Southern Pacific Railroads. Three similar machines, of 4,300hp with German transmissions, were also built for Southern Pacific by ALCO. In spite of impressive performances as haulers, the imported engines had technical features that were too failure-prone in the rugged American conditions, and by the early 1970s all were out of use. The native diesel traction industry had easily repelled the only serious foreign challenge it had met, or is likely to meet.

Top: The characteristic Alco outline seen on Union Pacific diesel units at Cheyenne, Wyoming. *Blackhawk Films*

Left: Two EMD GP-38s, Nos 3041 and 3042 of the Illinois Central, on freight. *Illinois Central Railroad*

Right: Three EMD E-type units head a Pennsylvania train out of Fort Wayne in December 1947. *Cecil J. Allen Collection*

RAILCARS AND LIGHTWEIGHTS

A NEW VERSION of an old concept caught the fancy of many railroads in the 1950s. Between the wars several American systems had operated single, self-propelled railcars on lightly-loaded country and suburban services, but by the early 1930s most had been discarded as uneconomical. A prime reason was that up to then technology had not yielded a power-plant that packed sufficient force in a compact size and weight; machinery that produced power took up too much of the space that should have been earning revenue.

The Second World War produced the solution to that problem and the big equipment manufacturers Budd seized the opportunity to exploit it. Budd had had a conviction that there was a future for railcars since the 1930s, but there was scant customer interest. Now it had the tool it had been looking for: the General Motors two-cycle V6 diesel engine and torque converter transmission evolved for US Army tanks. The whole assembly could be fitted under the floor of a railroad car; indeed there was room for two of these 275hp engines, so that in conjunction with lightweight bodywork fabricated of stainless steel, Budd was able to turn out a reversible, self-propelled railcar with the handsome power-to-weight ratio of 9hp to the ton. This was the ninety-seater RDC1 (RDC for Rail Diesel Car).

Budd was so confident that it had a vehicle which would appeal to railroads grappling with worsening losses in their passenger business that it set up an RDC production line before a single railcar had been sold. By 1952 it had already disposed of more than fifty RDCs and by the mid-1950s several railroads were happily discovering that railcars could virtually halve the cost of providing the same service with a locomotive-hauled train. Repair costs, in particular, were much lower. A significant factor in this saving was the ease with which the diesel engine could be disconnected from its fuel and other lines, then rolled out on a built-in trolley for attention on the workshop floor — there was no need for a workshop with an inspection pit for the job. A defective engine could be removed and replaced almost anywhere, and not necessarily by a highly skilled maintenance crew, in under two hours.

Before the 1950s were out Budd had sold over 350 RDCs of different types to North American railroads (and exported them too: the Commonwealth Railways of Australia ran one over the whole 1,051 miles of the Trans-Australian Railway from Port Augusta to Kalgoorlie in $19\frac{1}{4}$ hours). To suit varying customers' needs they were manufactured in five different marks, all but one on the same 85ft underframe and all but one powered by the standard pair of 275hp engines driving an axle on each bogie through an Allison torque converter. The pioneer RDC1 was a ninety-seater; the RDC2 was a seventy-one-seater with a baggage compartment, the RDC3 a forty-nine-seater with an area for baggage and mail sorting, the RDC4 a mail and baggage car on a 73ft 10in underframe, and the RDC9 a ninety-four-seater trailer with only one driving-cab and a single 300hp engine, designed to work in multiple with one of the other types of RDC.

The RDC was a lively performer. On level track it could reach its top speed within five miles of a standing start; and its disc brakes, backed up by an anti-slip device, could slow the car from 80mph to a stop within 1,900ft. That ideally suited the RDC to short-distance, multi-stop operation. The Baltimore & Ohio Railroad, which gave its RDCs the brand-name of Speedliners, could confidently time one on the Baltimore-Washington service to cover the 11.2 miles from Riverdale to Laurel in just nine minutes, representing an average speed of 74.7mph, although a line limit of 80mph was in force.

The most extensive user of RDCs was the Boston & Maine. Its Boston suburban services, which represented half the

system's passenger business by the mid-1950s, were losing money heavily. These services had almost the last steam trains on the road, and the B & M was anxious to abandon steam. Instead of buying replacement diesel locomotives, the B & M chose a twenty-five per cent more expensive investment in RDCs and a thorough reorganization of operation on its fifteen Boston suburban routes so that the railcars could be put to the best advantage.

At the peak of its RDC operation the B & M had over a hundred railcars, which it ran under the fleetname of Highliners. Since the 1950s forty per cent of the B & M's Boston local services have been cut out and the remainder are provided by B & M under contract to the Massachusetts Bay Transportation Authority (MBTA), which meets the shortfall on revenue. But at the start of 1977 B & M was still deploying around eighty RDCs, by then its only passenger equipment.

In the heyday of its RDC operation in the mid-1950s B & M was covering the Boston local network with fifty-five RDCs and a back-up of eight diesel locomotive-hauled train-sets (for the heaviest peak-hour workings), as against the seventy-five steam locomotives and 450 assorted and dilapidated passenger cars the previous timetable had demanded. Apart from the saving in sheer reduction of equipment, B & M found that, except when more than four fully powered RDCs of the earlier marks had to be coupled to provide adequate seating capacity, the average RDC's unprecedented running costs of around seventy-one cents a mile halved the previous steam train figure. A significant factor in this economy, of course, was the operational flexibility of the double-ended railcar, which substantially reduced terminal turnround costs. So dramatically were overhead costs cut that a good many

Left: An electric Metroliner built for high-speed New York – Washington service. *Williams & Meyer Company*

Top: A 'doodle-bug' – a Chesapeake & Ohio gas-electric car typical of many self-propelled vehicles in rural services in the 1930s. *W. A. Burke Jnr*

Above: A diesel railcar of the California Western RR at Willits, California, in August 1969. *J. K. Hayward*

RDCs actually cleared their purchase price (around $150,000 a car in the 1950s) within a year of entering service.

Several other railroads fully exploited the RDC's potential in commuter service, like the Pennsylvania-Reading Seashore Lines over the seventy to eighty miles from Camden City, New Jersey, to the

South Jersey coast. But many others put their RDCs to ambling rural runs that no rail vehicle could have made profitable. Few were assigned to inter-city working, though there was the remarkable case of the Western Pacific Railroad, which in 1950 acquired a pair of RDC2s to furnish a thrice-weekly 'Zephyrette' service over the 924 miles between Oakland and Salt Lake City. That lasted until the early 1960s, when Western Pacific sold the two railcars to Northern Pacific.

There was, however, one determined attempt to adapt the RDC to inter-city use in the North-East Corridor. In the mid-1950s several major railroads, principally in the east, were attracted to the energy-saving and hence cost-saving potential of unorthodox new forms of lightweight vehicle construction floated by equipment manufacturers. From abroad, the Spanish concern Talgo tried hard to establish a market in the United States for its patented low-centre-of-gravity, guided-axle, articulated four-wheel car. Rock Island Lines was persuaded to invest in a train-set for a two-round-trips-a-day service as the *Jet Rocket* between Chicago and Peoria in early 1956. Rock Island men were ecstatic at the initial results and soon scheming a sleeper version of the Talgo car for overnight working to Colorado, but the customers were not so enthusiastic. They condemned the diner and parlour of the *Jet Rocket*'s diminutive cars as claustrophobic by traditional North American standards, and within two years the Talgo train had been taken off the Peoria run in favour of conventional equipment. Similar reactions killed the four-wheeler Aerotrain which General Motors evolved for Union Pacific and which, as the *City of Las Vegas*, lasted less than a year from the end of 1956 to late 1957 on the Los Angeles-Las Vegas run.

Pullman-Standard produced a four-wheeler design which it branded Train X and captivated the celebrated Robert R. Young, then head of the Chesapeake & Ohio Railroad. When Young moved to the New York Central he took his liking for Train X with him, and in the summer of 1956 NYC launched the Pullman-Standard product on the Cleveland-Cincinnati route as the *Xplorer*. It ran up against the same customer reaction as the other lightweights and it, too, was removed from service within a year.

The most extravagant of the lightweight experimenters was the New York, New Haven and Hartford Railroads, then presided over by Patrick B. McGinnis — a man whose violin-playing hobby, in the context of the New Haven's disastrously ailing finances, prompted a good deal of satirical criticism. McGinnis idolized Robert R. Young: and Young was the most passionate advocate of lightweight trains as the cure for the worsening loss of money on North American inter-city rail passenger service. So McGinnis followed Young's lead, not just with one essay in the unorthodox, but three.

The New Haven adopted the Talgo

Right: The Pennsylvania Silverliner electric multiple-unit, which was based on Budd's lightweight Pioneer III, seen leaving Chestnut Hill for Philadelphia in June 1971. *V. Goldberg*

Below: A Canadian Pacific Dayliner on the CP subsidiary the Dominion Atlantic Railway at Kentville, Nova Scotia, in September 1972. *J. G. Tawse*

Bottom: Budd RDCs bring commuters into Boston's South station. *Brian J. Cudahy*

cars, but its Talgo set, named the *John Quincy Adams,* was as disparaged commercially and suspect technically as Rock Island's and it was soon discarded. Nevertheless, when McGinnis moved to Boston & Maine, (where his railroad career ended ignominiously with a 1965 jail sentence for accepting bribes on B & M equipment orders), he purchased another Talgo for B & M's Boston-Portland working. By the time he took delivery of this unit, B & M's traffic had contracted to such an extent that this Talgo unit, in white, blue and black livery, spent the whole of its short life on the Boston-Reading commuter shuttle.

For New Haven McGinnis also acquired a Train X set, which he assigned to the New York-Boston corridor run as the *Dan'l Webster.* Unusually for North America at the time, the *Dan'l Webster* was a double-ended push-pull, with a specially designed Baldwin-Lima-Hamilton diesel locomotive at each end of the set to cut terminal turnround time and costs. Another special feature of these locomotives was that, though they had hydraulic transmission for open mainline operation, their bogies were also fitted with electric traction motors and contact shoes so that they could be switched over to straight electric working, picking up current from the third rail, in the tunnelled approaches to New York's Grand Central terminal, where local ordinances prescribed steam and diesel traction.

Budd was the most enterprising of the US equipment manufacturers in the 1950s' exploration of unorthodox car-building. At the heavy end of the scale it devised the massive, twin-floor, Hi-Level cars for Santa Fe's *El Capitan.* For Pannsylvania it constructed the weight-saving Keystone stock, based on stainless steel bodies fabricated without the usual, heavy centre and side frame sills so that the central saloon could be sunk below wheel level between the bogies, and the centre of gravity lowered for greater stability at speed. Seven of these cars were built and survived to wear Amtrak colours.

Most promising of the Budd essays in the unconventional at this time was the Pioneer III, an extremely light and economically built car with an advanced new air-sprung, disc-braked bogie, which was designed so that its standard car-body could be easily and comparatively

cheaply adapted to the range of passenger service requirements, from ordinary coach to lounge, sleeper and diner. Possibly because of the disappointing record of other lightweight innovations, no railroad was bold enough to adopt the Pioneer III for inter-city hauls, but over sixty were built and very successfully used as commuter cars by the Pennsylvania and Reading systems.

For McGinnis of the New Haven, Budd developed in 1957 an inter-city RDC train-set, which it promoted as the *Hot Rod* (though New Haven gave it the more prosaic service name of *Roger Williams*). The six cars had the standard 85ft RDC underframes, but only the outer vehicles with streamlined ends were fitted with driving cabs. Every car had a pair of 300hp GM engines, so that the six-car set made up a total output of 3,600hp for its 375 tons — a very healthy power-weight ratio that gave it the ability to reach its maximum speed of 112mph within seven minutes of a standing start on level track using its main diesel-hydraulic power-plant. Like the locomotives of New Haven's *Dan'l Webster,* the *Hot Rod* also had low-power, back-up electric traction motors with third-rail pick-up shoes to take it into and out of New York.

Fitted with aircraft-style reclining seats and small refreshment counters in each head — end car, the *Hot Rod* was intended to link New York and Boston in less than three hours, five intermediate stops included.

Even before the New Haven subsided

Top: A 12-car rake of Budd RDCs on the Pennsylvania-Reading Seashore Lines. *Cecil J. Allen Collection*

Above: The short-lived 'John Quincy Adams' Talgo lightweight train of the New Haven, formed of single-axle cars articulated in triplets. *Cecil J. Allen Collection*

into its long-threatened financial quagmire, however, and several years before the Interstate Commerce Commission thrust New Haven's inter-state passenger services on to an unwilling Penn-Central in the mid-1960s, the *Roger Williams* set had been set aside along with the other New Haven lightweights. First it was stored, then dismantled into individual cars which were relegated to pool operation with New Haven's other, standard RDCs.

Many of RDCs are still at work in North America, on both sides of the 49th Parallel (Canadian National, which had forty-seven and called them Railiners, and Canadian Pacific, which acquired fifty-four and named them Dayliners, were among Budd's biggest customers for the railcars). But with rail passenger operation in the United States contracting, Budd failed to find any new RDC buyers after 1962. Amtrak thought of refurbishing some secondhand RDCs as snack-coaches or bar-lounges for economical inter-city shuttle working in populated corridors other than those in the north-east, but gave up the idea. The cars were growing too old and inevitably fault-prone — in fact, Amtrak had already had to supplant some of those it took over with locomotive-and-coach sets, as on the Chicago-Dubuque, Iowa, Blackhawk run.

Moreover, at the start of the 1970s Budd itself wanted to quit the rail car-building business after some financial shocks experienced in turning out new electric multiple-units and commuter cars. But the United States Justice Department vetoed a sale of this part of the Budd business to General Electric; and when the infant Amtrak started buying 500 new Amfleet coaches that were basically a copy of the Metroliner vehicles Budd had built for the New York-Washington corridor, to be mounted on Budd-style Pioneer III bogies, the Budd management had second thoughts and reopened its production lines.

By late 1976 Budd had regained sufficient enthusiasm to put on the market the outline of a second-generation RDC. For bodywork Budd proposed to adapt the Metroliner shell, which would be mounted on Pioneer III bogies and powered by a brace of GM 360hp truck diesel engines driving through a hydraulic twin disc torque converter transmission. That would give the vehicle a power-weight ratio of better than 10hp-ton, as all-up weight was unlikely to be much above 62-3 tons.

Budd drew up a versatile specification for the revived railcar, which was designated SPV-2000 (Self-Propelled Vehicle with a service life expectancy up to the year 2000 at least). The SPV-2000 could be offered with droop-snout streamlining and 120mph capability, or with flat-fronted end and 100mph top speed. It would be on offer with two engines, one only, or as a non-powered trailer; and it could be fitted out internally as a 109-seater commuter car, an eighty-four-seater inter-city car, a fifty-seater passenger and baggage car combine or as fifty-seater snack-bar-club coach. Compared with the price of $150,000 for the original RDC, Budd forecast that each SPV-2000 would cost a buyer around $750,000. Even so, Budd reckoned to attract customers for a minimum of 150 and perhaps as many as 350 within five years of proving and demonstrating a prototype, which was forecast to take the rails before the end of the 1970s.

Perhaps a new railcar age is about to open on North American railroads. Certainly Budd can take encouragement from Amtrak's contentment with its French-pattern Turboliner railcar sets — especially as Budd is certain that its SPV-2000 will consume only half the fuel of a Turboliner for a given passenger load and distance.

Top: In pre-Amtrak days, a Metroliner in Penn-Central livery. *J. K. Hayward*

Centre: New Haven's 'Roger Williams,' the inter-city train-set fashioned from Budd RDCs in 1957. *Cecil J. Allen Collection*

Bottom: Close-up of the Budd lightwieght Pioneer III coach showing the distinctive air-sprung truck. *Cecil J. Allen Collection*

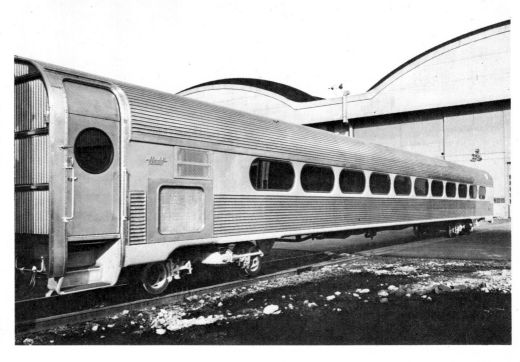

TURBINE LOCOMOTIVES & TURBOLINERS

FOR A TIME in the 1950s it seemed as if the diesel might have a rival. Wartime development had turned the turbine into a useful form of propulsion for aircraft. Might it not be equally serviceable in rail traction?

The technical attraction of the turbine, as distinct from the gas or diesel internal combustion engine, is its simplicity. In internal combustion, the gas expansion which creates power following combustion occurs in a fixed cylinder; the power has to be transmitted by the means of a piston moving in linear fashion, then transformed by crank into rotary motion. That involves many moving parts and interacting surfaces where problems of lubrication and wear can

arise. The turbine, on the other hand, is itself set in rotary motion by the combustion, so it has considerably fewer moving parts and should cost less for repair and maintenance. In addition, it is theoretically more efficient as an energy producer: it works on a higher air-to-fuel ratio, which should induce more complete combustion — and, incidentally, a cleaner exhaust.

There were attempts to marry old and new traction methods in steam turbine locomotives. Even before the Second World War General Electric had turned out two 2,500hp, steam turbine-electric units in which the steam turbine powered a generator of current for electric traction motors. Mounted on four bogies — two

two-axle unpowered and the other pair three-axle all powered — the turbine plant was housed in a typical cab-diesel-style body of the period. But after short trials, mostly on Union Pacific, both machines were consigned to scrap in 1942.

In 1946 the Pennsylvania Railroad was influenced by European developments to try a direct-drive steam turbine, a conventional-looking locomotive except for

Below: The final Union Pacific gas turbine design; an 8,500hp triple-unit of which thirty were built in 1958-61, with the driving cab and auxiliary plant as the lead unit, the turbine-generator in the centre, and the fuel tank as the final unit.
Union Pacific Railroad

its unlikely 6-8-6 wheel arrangement and lack of outside cylinders. It performed impressively in Pennsylvania express passenger service and once held an average of 105mph for thirty miles on level track with a 980-ton test load. But it was never multiplied and, suffering from the inevitable shortage of spares and repair cost of any one-off machine, the S-2 was overtaken by the advance of diesels.

Two other important ventures in the field were the huge coal-fired steam turbine electrics Baldwin conceived for the great coal carriers, Chesapeake & Ohio and Norfolk & Western Railroads. C & O's three were built in 1946-7 and each rated at 6,000hp. The locomotive and coal-bunker were carried on the same frame, with the bunker ahead of the driving-cab. The whole assembly was 140ft 3¾in long and carried on three idle two-axle and two powered four-axle bogies; with water-tender attached the assembly turned the scale at a gigantic 595 tons. Even allowing for C & O's anxiety to exploit the cheap and plentiful coal on its doorstep, its rash investment in not just one but three such untried and vastly expensive monsters was astonishing. The three machines lasted only until 1950, when C & O discarded all three as impossibly expensive in running and repair costs.

Undismayed, Norfolk & Western gave a final trial to the concept with its 586-ton *Jawn Henry,* built by Baldwin-Lima-Hamilton in conjunction with Westinghouse and boiler-makers Babcock & Wilcox in 1951. Essentially a freight hauler, unlike C & O's trio, the high-rpm, 4,500hp *Jawn* was miniature electricity generating station mounted on four three-axle powered bogies, and its heart was a high-pressure water-tube boiler with a chain grate unique in locomotive engineering. It used thirty per cent less coal than an orthodox steam engine, but some of its components were chronically troublesome; and it was handicapped by characteristic one-off problems. The last attempt to improve steam's efficiency as a hauler, big *Jawn* was retired at the beginning of 1958.

Union Pacific were the only railroad to register any success with turbine locomotives. In their machines the prime mover was the gas turbine. This takes in air, which it compresses and heats to about 500F°. Part of the air is mixed with oil in the form of a fine spray, ignited and heated six or seven times more in temperature, then reunited with the remaining air, which has bypassed the combustion chamber, to blast through the turbine as a mixture raised to over 1,000°F. After doing its turbine work, the hot gas is exploited to heat air newly taken in before it is released through an exhaust in the locomotive's roof. In a gas turbine-electric, such as Union Pacific adopted, the turbine drives a generator that supplies electric traction motors. For that, only a relatively small proportion of the turbine's output is available; the rest is absorbed in driving the air-compressor, as the turbine's consumption of air is enormous – hence the much bigger air-intakes in the flanks of a turbine locomotive than in a diesel. The attraction of gas turbine propulsion immediately after the Second World War was that it fed on Bunker C, a by-product of crude oil which was considerably cheaper than diesel oil and hence, in those days, a very inexpensive traction fuel indeed.

In 1948 General Electric, by then in marketing partnership with ALCO, constructed a 4,500hp gas turbine-electric demonstrator. Mounted on four two-axle bogies with all axles powered, it was externally a diesel locomotive apart from big bodyside air grilles. It was tested chiefly on the Union Pacific (whose livery it wore for most of its life, though it was always owned by General Electric). In nineteen months of trial, principally on the stiff inclines west of Cheyenne up to the 8,013 feet summit of Sherman Hill, the prototype's handling of 3,250-ton freights so impressed the UP that at the end of 1950 they ordered from General Electric ten of their own, virtually identi-

Below: One of the first series of Union Pacific gas turbines, a 4,500 single-unit of which ten were constructed in 1952. *Blackhawk Films*

cal with the demonstrator except that the production series had a single cab, whereas the prototype was double-ended. The vacated cab space was filled by an oil-bunker, but its 7,200 gallon capacity was quite inadequate and very soon Union Pacific had to hook tenders onto the turbine locomotives as additional 24,000 gallon fuel carriers. The turbine locomotives had to house other power-plant besides the turbine-generator set; a 200hp diesel-generator set was essential to start the turbine motoring (also to power one bogie's traction motors for manoeuvring the locomotive around depots and yards without extravagantly starting up its turbine), and a small steam generator was needed to keep the highly viscous oil-fuel flowing in all temperatures.

On the whole, the turbines proved very reliable on freight tonnage between Ogden (Utah), Cheyenne and Omaha, a route which includes the 7,230 feet Aspen Tunnel summit and Sherman Hill. UP therefore decided to order fifteen more, which were added to the stud in 1954. The only visual distinction between these and the first batch was that the newcomers had their bodysides gouged out to create a catwalk to the rear of the cab and alongside the machinery compartments.

The 4,500hp Union Pacific turbines served adequately through most of the 1950s. Towards the end of their career they were usually to be found with one or maybe two 2,000hp GP20 diesel road switchers hitched up behind their oil-tender, being remotely driven from the turbine's cab. Oddly, it was cheaper to run this multiple-unit combination throughout a turbine load-hauling journey than to stop the train and take on helpers only where they were needed. A turbine's efficiency and economy is largely dependent on its continuous working at full bore; to start up a turbine, or to have it idling on low power, is expensively wasteful of fuel (hence, of course, the Union Pacific locomotives' auxiliary diesel-generator set for yard work). So although the GP20s added little to the traction of a turbine-hauled UP freight train on level or slightly inclined track, to keep them permanently in tow was the most economical way of

providing for supplementary power in a crisis.

These first turbines were not powerful enough to count as replacements for Union Pacific's mammoth Big Boy 4-8-8-4 steam locomotives, however. To meet that requirement, in the late 1950s UP worked out with General Electric the design of a huge 8,500hp locomotive, of which thirty were built and taken into UP service between 1958 and 1961. They superseded the 4,500hp machines, which were traded-in with General Electric to provide the running gear and other equipment of the new 8,500hp locomotives.

With its ex-steam locomotive twelve-wheeled fuel-carrying tender included, the 8,500hp UP gas turbine-electric was a three-unit rig. The leading cab unit contained all the auxiliary plant, including an 850hp Cooper-Bessemer diesel-generator set to drive the turbine, excite the dynamic braking system and power all the traction motors of one unit for work in yards and depots. The second unit carried the turbine and generator. Both these main units were each carried on two six-axle bogies, with every axle powered— and on some of the series the tender-bogie axles were fitted with traction

motors as well. On these locomotives the fuel-oil was ready-heated by electricity.

Although these giants were increased to 10,000hp gross output after 1964, they still frequently took road switcher diesels for supplementary power. From time to time, too, a pair of the turbine outfits were coupled back to back to set up a 20,000hp multiple-unit hauler.

At the same time, diesel locomotive design and operating technology were developing. The power-weight ratio of diesel locomotives was being steadily improved and the gas turbine was losing its superiority in terms of output per ton of locomotive — an advantage that declined even more in view of the fact that the turbine only registered its maximum economy if it was hauling heavy tonnage on full power over a lengthy

Above: The extraordinary experimental coal-fired gas turbine intermittently tested on Union Pacific in 1962-63. *Cecil J. Allen Collection*

Below, left: One of Chesapeake & Ohio steam turbine-electrics of 1946-47, with the 'Sportsman', attacks the gradient out of Ashland, Kentucky. *Cecil J. Allen Collection*

Below, right: A United Aircraft three-car Turbotrain on trial for the US Department of Transportation. *United Aircraft Corporation*

period; at less than full throttle it became extravagant of fuel, so that it was operationally a rather inflexible traction unit. All this persuaded Union Pacific to change policy. From the mid-1960s they retired the big turbines and by the end of 1969 had taken all of them out of use. Their traction motors and bogies were re-used in the series of twin-engined 5,000hp U50C diesel road switchers that UP obtained from General Electric at the end of the 1960s.

One more experiment with turbine locomotives of this period deserves mention. For years the Bituminous Coal Institute had been wanting to see coal used as fuel for a gas turbine-electric locomotive, rather than oil (in the coal-fired Chesapeak & Ohio and Norfolk & Western Railroads' turbine locomotives described earlier the turbines were steam-driven; in this project the turbine propellant was to be combustion gases). In the late 1950s the Institute persuaded Union Pacific to collaborate as guinea-pig. The shell of a discarded Great Northern electric locomotive was acquired to carry the 5,000hp turbine (taken from one of the withdrawn 4,500hp locomotives), an ALCO 2,000hp Type PA-2 cab diesel was rebuilt to serve as the

lead control unit and auxiliary power, and to the rear was added a third unit housing the special coal pulverizer and fly ash separator gear which were essential to ensure that only pure gas reached the turbine. This extraordinarily ill-assorted and massive outfit took nearly three years to assemble, but eventually was ready for road trials in 1962. The tests were neither frequent nor encouraging and the contraption was soon put aside to lie idle for two or three years until it was dismantled in 1968.

Union Pacific apart, world interest in the turbine's rail traction potential stagnated during the 1950s, but by the mid-1960s the aerospace industry had revived it with a range of compact new gas turbines devised for helicopters and light aircraft. The aerospace industry itself worked hard to rouse this enthusiasm. From self-interest it was looking for new customers and diversification to insure against a reduction of expenditure on defence. It could also see the potential on railroads of an alliance of the new gas turbine technology and its lightweight aircraft construction techniques to produce an up-to-date version of the early diesel streamliner, though with a much higher power and more economical

power-ratio than, for example, the original Zephyrs.

In 1965, the Johnson administration gave encouragement to the railroads with its High Speed Ground Transportation Act, which set up demonstration projects in the North-East Corridor between New York and Washington, and New York and Boston, and also sponsored a contest for the design of a new high-speed train. Almost immediately United Aircraft Corporation entered the competition with a revolutionary five-car turbine-powered train-set which it had been working on since 1963. Compared with conventional equipment, the Turbotrain saved weight dramatically by substantial aircraft-style use of aluminium in the bodywork, combined with tubular steel for strength; by adopting a single-axle suspension like the unsuccessful Talgo and Aerotrain of a decade earlier; and by employing as prime mover an engine only 5ft long and $1\frac{1}{2}$ft in diameter. This engine was the UAC helicopter/turbo-prop 400hp ST6B gas turbine, arranged in groups to drive the road wheels mechanically via a gearbox.

UAC won a contract to supply two of these Turbotrains to the US Department of Transportation for trial; and tests began in late 1968. The following spring, public Turbotrain service was launched between New York and Boston with a service each way daily.

The most adventurous operator of the UAC Turbotrain was Canadian National, which procured five seven-car sets to operate a much accelerated service in its Toronto-Montreal corridor, where passenger traffic was predicted to double within a decade. The Turbotrains were to have entered public service in Canada's Centennial summer of 1967, but a succession of development problems delayed the start until the winter of 1968.

The launch was disastrous. Crippled by an almost instantaneous assortment of failures, the Turbos were withdrawn within weeks and returned to UAC for modification. Not until May 1970 did they re-enter Canadian National service. Yet again the Turbos were fault-prone and by mid-February of 1971 all five units were immobilized, to the accompaniment of some fairly acid public comment from UAC, who implied that

Canadian National was as good as halting the Turbos at the slightest engine cough or structural creak; to which a CN vice-president retorted that 'the trains never did measure up to the original contract and they haven't yet'. Less committed bystanders couldn't help wondering why the US Department of Transportation seemed to have so much less trouble with its New York–Boston Turbos.

Emphatically, the early Turbotrain difficulties were not attributable to the turbines; they showed very reasonable reliability and testified that their predicted economy in rail traction use was real. The root of the troubles (to recur in British Rail's Advanced Passenger Train development) was that too much bold innovation and aerospace technology had been crammed into the Turbotrain before each item's durability on rugged railroads had been put to the proof. Too much, from the transmission system and vehicle structure to the suspension and air-conditioning system, went virtually straight from drawing-boards to use on the track so far as railroad application was concerned.

Despite the chronic frustrations of services cancelled through failure, passengers took to the Turbotrains so much that the US Department of Transportation backed a continuation of the North-East Corridor demonstration project beyond the original terminal date of October 1970. Eventually, after a series of modifications to the gearboxes and rubber springing of the pendular suspension, and a comprehensive strengthening of the sound-insulation, the Canadians too were satisfied and the Turbos took up a virtually untroubled service there from the start of 1974.

In Europe, French Railways had made sure that they could walk before they tried to run in this new application of turbines. Taking the French-built Turbomeca two-shaft aerospace turbine, they first squeezed it into one of their standard diesel railcar sets for protracted testing at speeds up to 150mph. Satisfied on reliability and economy, and having

evolved an effective torque converter transmission system, in the summer of 1968 French Railways ordered their first ten Class ETG four-car gas turbine-hydraulic railcar units for revenue-earning service.

Unlike the United Aircraft Corporation Turbotrains, the French turbos were perfectly orthodox rail vehicles, apart from their turbine power-plant, based conservatively on the latest French Railways diesel railcars. Rated for a top speed of 112mph (but unable as yet to reach it because of track conditions), they looked perfect for passenger traffic on medium-distance routes where overall traffic potential would not warrant expensive electrification, but where there was passenger business to be won by a faster and more frequent passenger service. So, the turbos' 1970 debut on the Paris-Caen-Cherbourg route quickly produced the fastest journey time between **Paris and Caen, when the time for 148** miles was brought down to 109 minutes (average 81.4mph). Within a year revenue showed a twenty per cent rise.

Delighted, the French pressed ahead with a more powerful five-car unit, the RTG, motored by a 1,250hp Turmo III turbine-hydraulic power-car at each end, for longer and more difficult cross-country routes in their own country, like Lyons-Strasbourg and Lyons-Bordeaux. Across the Atlantic, Amtrak watched with interest. The export-hungry French were eager to serve; and in early 1973 an agreement was signed for two of the RTGs building for French Railways to be diverted to Amtrak on a two-year lease with an option to purchase both this pair and eight more.

The imports were launched on Amtrak's Chicago-St Louis route in the summer of 1973. In their first year they posted a ninety-two per cent reliability record in some 300,000 miles' revenue-earning service and boosted business by some fifty per cent. Eager for more, Amtrak requested a fleet of twenty RTGs, but the Department of Transportation refused permission for more than thirteen, including the two already in use. So four

more were built in France by ANF-Frangeco and delivered during 1975; the remaining seven, distinguishable by some altered external detail, were constructed in the United States under license from the French by Rohr Industries of California, which started deliveries at the end of 1976.

Rohr was another aerospace concern to diversify into railroad equipment and burn its fingers. Opening its account by winning the contract to build the Bay Area Rapid Transit (San Francisco) cars, it lost badly in executing this order and also its subsequent Washington Metro vehicle contract, which eventually cost around double the fixed price Rohr bid in 1972. Finally hit by a heavy cost over-run on the Amtrak Turbos — despite, it is said, charging well above the price of the French-built units — Rohr shut its railroad operations down in 1976 and surrendered the business to the old-established builders.

As well as Amtrak's Turboliners have performed, the Arab-Israeli war and the subsequent spectacular increases in oil prices have virtually ended turbine rail traction development in western Europe. Even the low-grade oil that fuels gas turbines is no longer a money-saving attraction. The dramatic shift in comparative energy prices has persuaded the French and other countries on the European mainland that, despite the high capital cost of installation, electrification from coal-fired generating plant is now the economical power medium for more lightly-trafficked routes where, a decade ago, oil seemed to be the only fuel. While the French have emphasized that they are happy to go on building gas turbine-powered equipment for export, they are very unlikely to breed new generations of Turboliners for their own system. So, if Amtrak decides to increase its basic Turboliner fleet, it might do so in isolation.

Below: Pennsylvania's direct-drive steam turbine 6-8-6 of 1946 at speed. It was reputed to have held 105mph for thirty miles of level track with a 980-ton test train. *Cecil J. Allen Collection*

ZEPHYRS AND HIAWATHAS, Chiefs and Rockets, Daylights and 400s, Florida Specials and countless Limiteds – all were household names in America in the nineteen-thirties, 'forties and 'fifties. Each such title, with an appropriate prefix, denoted some crack passenger train, sometimes involving more than one railroad.

Pride of place must go to the Zephyrs, the first of which was a modest affair. It comprised a three-car train-set, articulated throughout and carried on four trucks. The leading vehicle was a 600hp locomotive whose power unit was a Winton 201A diesel engine mounted integrally with the bogie. Weighing under 100 tons, the three-car train carried seventy-two passengers in its two trailer cars. The car-bodies were of fluted stainless-steel construction and were built by the Budd Company in Philadelphia. The train was given the name *Pioneer Zephyr*. It was built early in 1934 and displayed in Chicago at the Century of Progress Exposition that year after the epoch-making demonstration run and endurance test of 1,015 miles from Denver to Chicago.

After more demonstration runs, towards the end of 1934 the train entered revenue-earning service between Kansas City, Omaha, and Lincoln, Nebraska, a run of 250 miles. A similar train-set, but with a second-class coach seat section (instead of baggage space) in the rear end of the leading (power) car, went into service between Boston and Portland, Maine, in 1935 for the Boston & Maine and Maine Central railroads. That one was named *Flying Yankee* and is now preserved at Edaville, about forty miles from Boston. The *Pioneer Zephyr* is also preserved, at the Chicago Museum of Science & Industry.

The *Pioneer Zephyr* was followed in 1935 by three more train-sets. The first two, still of three cars each, seated eighty-eight and entered service as *Twin Zephyrs* in April between Chicago and the Twin Cities (St Paul and Minneapolis), taking six and a half hours for the 437-mile journey. Their route was markedly longer than the two alternatives, those of the Milwaukee Road (421 miles) and of the Chicago & North Western Railway (407 miles). The third new train was of four passenger cars, seating ninety-two, and an additional baggage-mail car. It became the *Mark Twain Zephyr*, running between St Louis and Burlington, Iowa, 221 miles, in five and three-quarter hours

Below: The 'California Zephyr' at Denver Union station behind five EMD F diesels of Denver & Rio Grande Western in June 1969. *V. Goldberg*

with a number of stops. Later, from 1941, this route was also covered by the *Zephyr-Rocket*, an overnight train between St Louis, Burlington and Minneapolis, using Rock Island tracks north of Burlington on the 585 mile run to the Twin Cities, a fourteen-hour journey.

More Zephyrs appeared towards the end of 1936, when two 1,800hp locomotive units, named *Pegasus* and *Zephyrus*, entered service on the Chicago-Twin Cities run, with seven-car trains, each set making a round trip daily. The original *Twin Zephyr* three-car trains were found new tasks elsewhere on the Burlington system. One became the *Sam Houston Zephyr*, running the 283 miles between Fort Worth, Dallas and Houston in five hours. The other set became the *Ozark State Zephyr*, between St Louis and Kansas City (279 miles).

Also in 1936 there were the two train-sets which formed the original *Denver Zephyrs*. Each partly articulated train was hauled by a two-unit locomotive totalling 3,000hp. The pairs of locomotives were named *Silver King/Silver Queen* and *Silver Knight/Silver Princess*, respectively. Each of the twelve-car trains included coaches, a dining-car, four sleepers and an observation car, as well as a crew dormitory-passenger lounge car and a combined power-generator-postal-baggage car. The *Denver Zephyrs* unquestionably provided facilities which set standards for twenty years or more, including such novelties as tight-lock couplers, double glazing, foam-rubber seats and electric razor power points. The passenger cars were named, using the common prefix *Silver* – because of the unpainted stainless-steel outer panelling, which was to become a familiar feature of many streamlined trains in years to come. The trains entered daily overnight service with an exacting sixteen-hour schedule for the 1,034-mile Chicago-Denver run.

In 1939, the 1,000hp locomotive *Silver Charger*, the last to be styled in similar fashion to the *Pioneer Zephyr* (as were all those mentioned so far) entered service with the *General Pershing Zephyr* on the St Louis-Kansas City run. Two other pre-war Zephyrs were the *Silver Streak Zephyr* between Kansas City and Lincoln (the route of the *Pioneer Zephyr*) and, later in the year, the *Texas Zephyr*, running 834 miles, between Denver and Dallas over the Colorado & Southern lines. Not all of the Zephyrs introduced after the 1936 train-sets were wholly of stainless steel. Some trains included refurbished sleeping-cars of earlier heavyweight pattern.

Eventually the earliest of the epoch-making diesel trains became outdated; by 1942 the *Pioneer Zephyr* had moved to the secondary Lincoln-Hastings-McCook service, making local stops over part of the *Denver Zephyr* route. The Chicago Burlington & Quincy Railroad was first to introduce the now familiar Vista-dome coach, in 1947, in what might be termed the third generation of twin-Zephyr trains. The 1936 train-sets so displaced from the Twin Cities run moved to

the eastern half of the Chicago-Denver route, providing fast daytime service between Chicago, Omaha and Lincoln, some 557 miles, taking about eleven hours for the run with around twenty stops.

The high point of the Zephyr era came in 1949 with the introduction of the *California Zephyr*. This train, often with five dome-cars in its formation, ran between Chicago and Oakland (for San Francisco), about 2,525 miles. As far as Denver, Burlington Railroad tracks were used. West of Denver the spectacular Moffat tunnel route of the Denver & Rio Grande Western Railroad was followed; up through the front range of the Rockies

Above right: The 'California Zephyr' with Western Pacific diesels at Oakland and, right, on Denver & Rio Grande metals at Helper, Utah; in June 1969. *V. Goldberg*

Below: Diesels of the Burlington head the 'Kansas City Zephyr' past Naperville, Illinois. *Blackhawk Films*

Bottom: Another scene at Naperville as the domes of the 'California Zephyr' glide by after their long run from San Francisco to the Midwest. *Blackhawk Films*

and then west via Western Pacific Railroad across Utah and Nevada and down the scenic Feather River canyon to Sacramento and on to Oakland. Whereas the other Zephyrs had combined speed and comfort, the schedule of the *California Zephyr* was arranged so that, in each direction, the two most scenic sections were traversed in daylight on the two days and two nights of the run. For years, the train ran completely filled day after day, but rising cost, rather than declining patronage, caused its discontinuance in 1970.

In the early nineteen-fifties still more Zephyrs were introduced, including a new daytime Chicago-Kansas City train (466 miles), the *Kansas City Zephyr*. It had an overnight counterpart in the *American Royal Zephyr*. The *Ak-Sar-Ben Zephyr* (Nebraska spelled backwards) gave overnight service on the Chicago-Omaha-Lincoln run; it received new rolling stock in the early 'fifties. The ultimate Zephyr train-sets came in 1956 when two superlative fourteen-car trains

were introduced on the trunk Chicago-Denver route; they displaced the two trains built in 1936, which were then moved to the *Texas Zephyr* route and the new trains took up the title of *Denver Zephyr*. Each of the new train-sets included three dome-cars – one a coach, one a buffet car – and at the rear a dome-lounge for first-class (sleeper) passengers. Each train-set also included two slumber-coaches, which introduced second-class enclosed sleeping-berths.

Most of the new types of cars from the 1956 trains went into Amtrak service, but not necessarily on Zephyr duty. Two Zephyrs survived into the late nineteen-seventies. The Denver & Rio Grande Western, one of the railroads which chose not to hand its passenger trains over to Amtrak in 1971, decided when the *California Zephyr* was cancelled, to continue at least a rump of *Californian Zephyr* service with *CZ* equipment. In the spring of 1970, therefore, the D & RGW inaugurated a thrice-weekly *Rio Grande Zephyr* between Denver and Salt Lake

Above: Eastbound and westbound 'California Zephyrs' meet in Glenwood Canyon, on the Denver & Rio Grande Western, where the idea of vista-domes was born.
Denver & Rio Grande Western Railroad

City. The only relic of Zephyr service in Amtrak's rosters is the *San Francisco Zephyr* which runs daily from Chicago to Denver and Ogden over the Union Pacific and thence to Oakland over the Southern Pacific Railroads.

It is still possible to ride on an original Zephyr – in Saudi Arabia, not in the USA. Twenty-one Zephyr cars, including the celebrated diner-observation car, were reconditioned and sold to the Saudis by the Chicago Burlington & Quincy Railroad in the 1960s. Today, there is a regular Zephyr service over the 350-mile line between Dammam on the Persian Gulf and the Saudi capital Riyadh, over a railway constructed for the late King Ibn Saud by the Arabian-American Oil Co.

Great Streamliners
THE HIAWATHAS

IN THE LATE 1930s passenger train services in the United States reached the highest level of speed and comfort in their history. Recovery from the disastrous trade slump at the beginning of that decade had been rapid; competition from motorways and air services was only just beginning to be felt; and public response to improved railway facilities had been sufficiently encouraging for the railways to invest considerable sums in new rolling stock and motive power. The diesel invasion was then still in its infancy, and steam was still being relied on for most of the fastest passenger services in the country.

All the railways in the USA were privately owned, and in many directions were keenly in competition with each other. This applied to the three services connecting Chicago with the Twin Cities of St Paul and Minneapolis, which were all roughly equal in length. They were those of the Chicago, Burlington & Quincy; the Chicago, Milwaukee, St Paul & Pacific; and the Chicago & North Western Railways. The last two served intermediately the important city of Milwaukee, but the fairly densely populated country between the terminals of each route also contained a number of good-sized towns at which stops helped to swell the passenger complements of the principal expresses. The Burlington route measured 427 miles in length from Chicago to St Paul; the Milwaukee line 410 miles; and the North Western, the shortest of the three, 396 miles.

Up to 1934 a journey between Chicago and St Paul or Minneapolis usually involved night travel; the one or two day trains by each route took about ten hours. By then motorways had made 50mph road journeys possible between these cities, and road competition was beginning to cut into railway patronage. In that year both the Milwaukee and the North Western companies conducted some speed experiments over their well-aligned routes between Chicago and Milwaukee, a distance of eighty-five miles in each case, in preparation for acceleration.

So it was that on 20 July 1934 steam locomotive 4-6-4 No 6402 of the Milwaukee Road headed a special five-coach train of 347 tons, which covered the eighty-five miles in 67 minutes 35 seconds, at a start-to-stop average of 75.5mph. Once clear of the speed

restrictions through the suburbs of both cities, an average of 89.9mph was maintained over 68.9 miles of the journey and a maximum of 103½mph was attained — one of the fastest runs that had been made with steam power in the USA to that date. The startling result of the series of tests was the announcement that from early in 1935 all three competing routes would cut the times of their fastest trains between Chicago and the Twin Cities from ten to six and a half hours. While the Burlington authorities decided on diesel power for their new trains, the Milwaukee for a number of reasons decided to keep to steam, as did the

North Western. The latter was content to operate with standard equipment, but in 1934 the Milwaukee had made its high-speed intentions clear by ordering from the American Locomotive Company two 4-4-2 locomotives of an entirely new type — probably the last Atlantic steam design in world railway history.

In the meantime, in accordance with American practice, names had to be thought out for the new trains. The Chicago & North Western, with a route of round about 400 miles to be covered in roughly the same number of minutes, decided on *Twin Cities 400*, and followed up with a number of other *400s* over

pressure was 300lb per sq in. The weight of the locomotive in working order was 125 tons, of which 62½ tons were available for adhesion. The ten-wheel tenders carried 4,000 gallons of fuel-oil and 13,000 gallons of water and weighed 110½ tons.

A streamlined shroud covered each locomotive, which was the more striking in appearance because of its livery — a broad orange band, edged with crimson, extending from above the front pilot, or cowcatcher, round both sides of the engine to the cab, the sides of which with the tender were orange from top to bottom. The boiler-casing was a light brownish grey, and round the front of the engine it carried handsome stainless steel wings, with a large number on a red ground in the centre and the standard American headlight. Above the boiler was a black casing, which concealed the chimney and other boiler mountings. The special coaches built for the service also shared the crimson-lined orange livery.

The *Hiawatha* started its revenue-earning career in August 1935. It began as a six-coach formation. Next to the engine came a restaurant-buffet, which included what was probably the first cocktail bar to be introduced on an American train and also a 'Tip Top Tap' room. Then came three open 'coaches', followed by a Pullman parlour car and a beaver-tail observation car. At a later date the buffet-restaurant was transferred to a more easily accessible location in the centre of the train.

At first the *Hiawatha* made one trip in each direction daily. There were five intermediate stops, and the booked average speeds between them westbound were 68.0, 66.4, 71.8, 66.7, 55.2 and 59.4mph; travelling east the corresponding speeds from St Paul were 58.5, 55.2, 69.0, 73.9, 67.2 and 68.0mph. The whole journey of 410 miles, five stops included, was completed in six and a half hours in each direction, at an average of 63.1mph. The new Atlantics were quick to show their paces. On a test run on 15 May 1935, with a complete *Hiawatha* train-set, No 1 covered the 136 miles from Milwaukee to New Lisbon in 115 minutes at an average of 74.9mph, reaching a top speed of 112.5mph. The new schedule, however, had contemplated a maximum speed of only about 90mph, though speeds up to 100mph were acceptable if necessary for time-keeping. Eventually the cant of the track on many curves was increased sufficiently to make 100mph speeds quite comfortable for passengers.

On 29 May 1935 the *Hiawatha* entered revenue service, and was an immediate success. Soon its patronage was exceeding that of the competing North Western *400s* and Burlington *Zephyrs*, carrying well over 200 passengers daily; a month after its inauguration a fourth second-class coach was added, and a month later a fifth, making the train up to eight vehicles. Duplicate trains had to be run at weekends, and two more Atlantics, Nos 3 and 4, joined the first

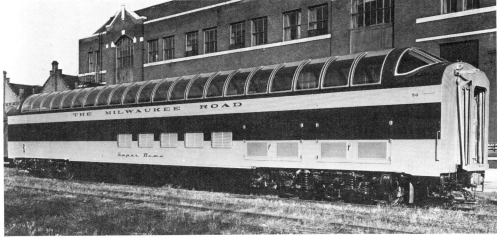

Left: Head-on view of one of the superb Class F7 streamlined 4-6-4s built for the 'Hiawatha' service in 1938. *Cecil J. Allen Collection*

Top: Headed by an F7 4-6-4, the 'Hiawatha' approaches Milwaukee, Wisconsin, in August 1941. *R. H. Kindig*

Above: One of ten full-length Super Domes built by Pullman-Standard for the 'Hiawatha' services in 1952. Six of them were sold to Canadian National in 1964; the remainder eventually passed into Amtrak hands. *Chicago, Milwaukee, St Paul & Pacific Railroad*

various main lines which had no similar 400-mile qualification. The Burlington chose the title *Twin Cities Zephyr*, and diesel-operated Zephyrs became a feature of Burlington operation from that time on. The Milwaukee management thought first of 'Flash', but a suggestion from the Mechanical Engineer's office of *Hiawatha*, after Longfellow's legendary Indian who was fleet of foot, gave the line the title it was seeking.

The new Milwaukee Atlantics, Nos 1 and 2, were delivered in May 1935. The class was oil-fired and had 7ft coupled wheels and 19in by 28in cylinders; the firegrate area was 69sq ft, heating surfaces totalled 3,245sq ft, superheating surface was 1,029sq ft and working

two. In its first year of operation the *Hiawatha* earned $700,000 clear of operating expenses, interest and depreciation. A brand new set of coaches appeared in 1936, and yet another in 1938, each more luxurious than its predecessor, and passenger patronage steadily increased; by 1936 an average of 723 passengers was being carried by the two *Hiawathas* daily. On 6 October 1938, after forty months, the total number of passengers reached the million mark.

The limit load for the Atlantics on the scheduled timings had been set at nine coaches, and it became clear that with passenger patronage steadily growing, greater locomotive power would be needed. Consequently, in September 1938 there appeared the first of a new F7 Hudson 4-6-4 class – one of the finest locomotives both in appearance and performance that ever graced American metals. The 7ft coupled wheels of the Atlantics were retained, but cylinder dimensions were increased to $23\frac{1}{2}$in by 30in, firegrate area was increased to 96.5sq ft, the heating surface went up to 4,166sq ft and superheating surface to 1,695sq ft. Working pressure remained at 300lb per sq in. Weight in working order of $185\frac{1}{2}$ tons included $96\frac{1}{2}$ tons adhesion. Coal (automatically fired) was substituted for oil as fuel and the twelve-wheel tender, accommodating twenty-five tons of coal and 20,000 gallons of water, weighed $167\frac{1}{2}$ tons. In running order, engine and tender turned the scale at 353 tons.

The performance of these remarkable machines on the track became almost legendary. On one journey, with a nine-coach train of 385 tons, No 100 cut the 75-minute schedule for the eighty-five miles from Milwaukee to Chicago to 69 minutes 27 seconds, including the necessarily rather slow running through the outskirts of Milwaukee and the suburbs into Chicago, and a 50-mph slow passage through Rondout. Over practically level track thirty-one consecutive miles were covered at 100mph or over, with a maximum of 110mph. Another of the Hudsons was once called on in an emergency to handle two night sleeping-car trains coupled together, and worked the resulting enormous 1,905-ton train from a dead start up to 70mph in no more than twelve miles of level track.

By 1939 duplications of the *Hiawathas* to cope with public demand were becoming so frequent that it was decided to run a *Morning Hiawatha* and an *Evening Hiawatha* in each direction daily. The westbound morning train was slower than the other three, as it was scheduled to make sixteen regular and two conditional stops between Chicago and St Paul, and so took 7 hours 50 minutes for the run, though it shared in the common 75-minute booking for the eighty-five miles from Chicago to Milwaukee. By January 1940 the fastest overall time came down to six and a quarter hours for the 410 miles between Chicago and St Paul, and the eastbound *Morning Hiawatha* set up a new record by being booked over the 78.3 miles

from Sparta to Portage in fifty-eight minutes, to make an average of 81mph. It thus became the only train in world history that was ever scheduled at over 80mph from start to stop with steam power. Equally the Hiawathas were the only expresses ever required to run at 100mph with steam locomotives.

But the reign of the magnificent Type F7 4-6-4s was to be cut short. On 20 September 1941, almost three years to the day after the first F7 had headed one of the *Hiawatha* trains, events cast the first shadow over the Hudsons – the appearance at the head of the *Morning Hiawatha* at Minneapolis of two Electromotive diesels giving 4,000hp that heralded the ultimate take-over of all the *Hiawatha* services by diesel power.

By then, however, the public reaction to the speed and luxury of *Hiawatha* travel had become so favourable that similar trains had been introduced over other parts of the Milwaukee system. In 1936 the North Woods area of Wisconsin, which until then had been served by connection with the Twin Cities at New Lisbon, got its own through *North Woods Hiawatha* between Chicago and Minocqua. The *Chippewa Hiawatha*, taking another route northward from Milwaukee, parallel to Lake Michigan and terminating at Ontonagon on Lake Superior, was introduced the following year. Next, in 1940, came the *Mid-West Hiawatha*, with an eight-hour run between Chicago and Omaha that boldly challenged the Chicago & North Western and the Burlington services between those cities, and carried a through portion, detached at Manilla, for Sioux City.

More important than all of them was the *Olympian Hiawatha*, a through express over the 2,207 miles between Chicago and Seattle, with a through section for Tacoma, introduced in 1947. The forty-five-hour journey of this express required six complete twelve-car trains for its daily maintenance in both directions, including, of course, various types of sleeping accommodation, and the dome-observation cars that were becoming common on American long-distance trains. The *Olympian* was also the only *Hiawatha* to require electric haulage over part of its route, as the 438 miles of the main line through the Rockies between Harlowton and Avery, Montana, were electrically worked. Over the remainder of the route three-unit diesels of 6,000hp were required.

Rolling stock displaced from the original *Hiawatha* trains by the introduction of new and still more luxurious sets were used to form various later services, though large numbers of new coaches also had to be built to satisfy the demand. Similarly, as the Atlantics and the Hudsons gave way to diesels between Chicago, Milwaukee, St Paul and Minneapolis, they found plenty of employment on the other *Hiawatha* trains, supplemented by older 4-6-2 and 4-6-0 locomotives which were decorated for the purpose with *Hiawatha* colours and given partial streamlining.

Needless to say, the 4,000hp (later

4,500hp) diesel locomotives groups had no difficulty in maintaining the fast *Hiawatha* schedules between Chicago and Milwaukee. On one run with a nine-coach load the time over the eighty-five miles was cut to 64½ minutes start to stop – 79.1mph average – with the 62.7 miles between Signal Tower A-68 and Tower A-5 covered in just under 39 minutes at 96.2mph average. In the later part of the Second World War and the years immediately following, passenger traffic was so heavy that the Twin Cities Hiawathas loaded at times to fourteen or fifteen coaches.

Before long, however, the decline began to set in. In the 1960s the various *Hiawathas* began to disappear, one of the first being the *Olympian*, in 1961, after a reign of no more than fourteen years. A steady deceleration also set in.

Amtrak operates two trains over *Hiawatha* territory, but on schedules that are a shadow of the former *Hiawatha* performance. In the spring of 1977 a com-bination of dilapidated Milwaukee Road track and the tendency of Amtrak's big six-axle SPD40F diesels to spread the rails and derail themselves on curves had enforced 40mph or even lower speed limits over much of the bends between Milwaukee and St Paul. As a result, Amtrak's *Empire Builder* was retimed over the 421 miles from Chicago to Minnea-polis in 10 hours 20 minutes, inclusive of six intermediate stops, a distance for which the steam-powered *Hiawatha* of the early 1940s required only 6¼ hours. For the whole of its 2,287-mile trip from Chicago to Seattle the *Empire Builder* was taking 49 hours 55 minutes.

The *Empire Builder*, running daily each way, perpetuates a title used by the former Great Northern Railway, now part of Burlington Northern, for the sumptu-ous Chicago-Seattle streamliner it in-augurated in 1947. Amtrak rerouted the train via Milwaukee at the eastern end of its run, since the traditional Chicago Burlington & Quincy route eastward from the Twin Cities served no significant commercial centre, and for a while gave it the *Hiawatha* name between Chicago and Minneapolis to match its use of the *Hiawatha* track between these two cities. Now it is *Empire Builder* throughout its itinerary, which from Minneapolis fol-lows the Great Northern route via Minot and Havre between Fargo and Spokane, and on from Spokane to Seattle.

The GN-route train became exclusively the *Empire Builder* when Amtrak restored a second daily service between Chicago and Minneapolis. This is now the *Hia-watha* – if only in name. Three days a week it is extended, as the *North Coast Hiawatha*, from Minneapolis to Seattle over the former Northern Pacific (now Burlington Northern) track via Billings between Fargo and Spokane, and thence to Seattle. Like the *Empire Builder,* and for the same dismal reasons, it was drastically decelerated in the spring of 1977 to take 50½ hours over the 2,228-mile run from Chicago to Seattle.

Left: A Milwaukee 2-D-D-2 electric 'Little Joe', so called because the type was built for a cancelled Second World War order for Soviet Russia. *G. G. M. Robinson*

Below: Inside the Skytop lounge of the Hiawatha' in 1948.
Chicago, Milwaukee, St Paul & Pacific Railroad

Bottom: The Skytop lounge brings up the rear of the 'Olympian Hiawatha' en route from Chicago to Seattle at Three Forks.
Cecil J. Allen Collection

Great Streamliners
THE TWENTIETH CENTURY LIMITED

FOR MANY YEARS, no tourist in the United States could say that his stay had been complete unless he had 'ridden the *Century*'. Today, alas, the experience is no longer possible. The *Twentieth Century Limited* was one of the earliest victims of the drastic curtailment of American passenger services that resulted from air and road competition.

The service began in June 1902 when the New York Central & Hudson River Railroad and the Lake Shore & Michigan Southern Railroad introduced an express service over their joint 961-mile route between New York and Chicago; the twenty-hour schedule cut four hours from the previous best over the course. The new train was named *Twentieth Century Limited*. As the names of the two railways indicated, for the first 142 miles, to Albany, the NYC & HRR main line, lieing due north, ran along the left bank of the Hudson River. At Albany the line turned due west through Syracuse to a course just south of Lakes Ontario and Erie, through Buffalo, where the LS & MSRR took over, to Cleveland and Toledo. Then a cut across country brought the line into Chicago, at the southern end of Lake Michigan.

The proximity of the railway to the water over most of its length prompted the New York Central solgan, 'Water Level Route – You Can Sleep', which the NYC splashed over its timetables and other publicity. The slogan was also a sly dig at the competing Pennsylvania Company, whose *Pennsylvania Special* (in 1912 renamed the *Broadway Limited*), was introduced on the same day as the *Twentieth Century Limited* and on the

same twenty-hour schedule. The Pennsylvania took a shorter 908-mile course through the Allegheny mountains, at the cost of climbing to a summit level of 2,193 feet at Gallitzin, west of Altoona, up gradients as steep as one in fifty, with correspondingly hard effort and noisy exhaust by the locomotives.

Development of the *Twentieth Century* route was undertaken by the New York Central System, an amalgamation of the New York Central and the Lake Shore lines. In later years the route had the distinction of being the longest four-track main line in the world; there were 474 miles of it continuously from Castleton, just outside New York, to Collinwood, in the suburbs of Cleveland. More recently, however, much of the quadruple track has been reduced to ordinary double track, but with frequent cross-over roads and suitable signalling to permit either-way working on both lines.

By contrast, in former days when the *Twentieth Century Limited* and other expresses reached Syracuse, their route to the passenger station lay, like a tramway, through busy city streets at 15mph, until at long last a new main line running into a new station made it possible to abandon this troublesome practice. Steam

haulage throughout of the *Twentieth Century* for the first five years of its life gave way in 1907 to electric operation between the Grand Central Terminal in New York and Wakefield, extended in 1913 to Harmon, nearly thirty-three miles out.

The cut of four hours below the previous fastest time between New York and Chicago, initiated with the *Twentieth Century Limited,* introduced a novel system of fare charging. With the previous twenty-eight hours fixed as the standard time, an extra fare of one dollar (later increased to $1.20) was charged for every hour that the passenger saved with the accelerated service. With every subsequent acceleration the supplement was increased, but with the proviso that for every hour that the *Twentieth Century* might be late in arriving, the passenger was entitled to a corresponding refund. In later years, however, this flexible fare system was replaced by a flat-rate service charge, in addition to the first-class fare and Pullman supplement.

Mention of Pullman brings its reminder that the *Twentieth Century Limited* was an all-Pullman train. In its early days the coaches were of the Pullman convertible type. Gradually, however, new Pullman

stock, the rear-end observation platforms on the last coach were being superseded by glassed-in observation lounges, and others kinds of amenities were being introduced.

In the middle 1950s the *Twentieth Century Limited* had reached the height of its fame. It had become one of a number of 'all-room' trains. The least expensive accommodation was in roomettes, which were tiny single rooms, dovetailed into one another to make the maximum possible use of car space. They provided comfortable seats for daytime travel and a quick-action fold-down ready-made-up bed, with their own toilet facilities. Then there were single bedrooms, similarly with beds folding into the walls, but with rather more space; still larger double bedrooms for couples; and 'master' rooms', which were suites with their own shower-baths.

The complete normal formation of the *Twentieth Century* in its heyday included four drawing-rooms, four 'compartments', seventy-nine double bedrooms and thirty roomettes, providing sleeping accommodation for just over 200 passengers in nine coaches. In addition there were two restaurant cars, a club lounge, a baggage car with sleeping-

Left: Final steam power of the 'Century'; a New York Central streamlined Hudson 4-6-4, No 5448, approaches Chicago with an ordinary train in September 1939. *R. H. Kindig*

Above: Rear of the Budd stainless-steel 'Twentieth Century Limited' train-set at Bear Mountain bridge in August 1963. *W. E. Zullig*

cars were introduced with single and double rooms of various sizes (some oddly described as 'drawing-rooms'), and the supplementary Pullman charges were varied according to the size and relative luxury of the accommodation provided. By 1908 wooden coach-bodies were being replaced by all-steel

accommodation for off-duty train staff, and a post office and 'express' (parcels) car. Refreshments could be obtained in a couple of the train lounges as well as in the dining-cars.

The size of the staff required to man such a hotel-on-wheels included the dining and refreshment car attendants, kitchen crew, a 'porter' for each sleeping-car, baggage-men, conductor, barber, lady hostess, even a train secretary, and, of course, the enginemen. It could easily run to a total of thirty of more; the need for a special service charge is thereby explained.

For some years the sleeping-cars included two which were transferred in Chicago from the New York Central to the Santa Fe Railroad, and worked by Santa Fe *Super-Chief* train through to Los Angeles, and thus across the United States from the Atlantic to the Pacific coast. But, in time, air competition put the Los Angeles sleepers out of business, and also reduced the New York-Chicago clientele until at last, by the middle 1960s, the proud all-Pullman *Twentieth Century* had been invaded by sleeper coaches. Also added were reclining-chair cars — that is, open saloons fitted with tilting seats to ease night-time travel — available, like single and double rooms of the sleeper coaches, at second-class fares with supplementary and the flat service charges added. This extension of facilities

did not generate an economic revival and turned out to be only the prelude to the final withdrawal of the *Twentieth Century Limited* in 1970.

In its earlier years the train was not unusually operated in three or more sections; indeed, as many as eight sections of the one train were known to follow one another along the 961-mile route. Later on, additional named trains with but little longer journey times relieved the pressure on the *Century*, as also did the splitting off of the Boston

portion, attached and detached at Albany, into a separate train called the *New England States*. By degrees the stops at Albany and Syracuse, going west, became halts to pick up passengers only, and at Buffalo no passenger business was done. The previous stop and reversal at Cleveland Union Terminal was cut out by the use of an avoiding line, reducing the overall journey to 958 miles; and the Toledo and Elkhart stops were restricted to setting down only, with corresponding arrangements in the reverse direction.

Below: With the 'Century's' new stock of the mid-1950s there came the roomette which included its own lavatory, individual heating and air-conditioning controls. *Ian Allan Library*

Bottom: Richly furnished Pullman observation car which was introduced to the 'Century' in 1929. *Ian Allan Library*

Right: The diesel-powered 'Twentieth Century Limited' alongside the Hudson River. *Cecil J. Allen Collection*

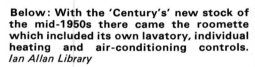

From its introductory schedule in 1902 of twenty hours in each direction, the *Twentieth Century Limited* was accelerated in 1908 for a brief period to eighteen hours. It was only a brief improvement however, and after a serious accident to the rival *Pennsylvania Special,* whose time also had been cut to eighteen hours, there was a reversion to the twenty-hour schedule. So matters continued until April 1932, when an eighteen-hour booking was again essayed, but a year later that was cut to seventeen and three-quarter hours. In June 1938 a further reduction to sixteen hours for the first time brought the overall speed of the *Twentieth Century* up to 60mph, all stops included. In the early part of the Second World War there was a temporary increase to seventeen hours, but the sixteen-hour schedule was restored in the spring of 1946, by which time diesel power had come in to replace the steam locomotives.

Even the twenty-hour schedule involved some very fast intermediate times.

In the final years the *Century* was booked in both directions over the 133 miles between Toledo and Elkhart in 111 minutes at 71.9mph start to stop; from Buffalo to Collinwood (there was a stop outside Cleveland to change engine crews) the time allowed for the 174.7 miles was 147 minutes and in the reverse direction 148 minutes, at start-to-stop averages of 71.3 and 70.9mph respectively. Buffalo-Collinwood was the longest non-stop part of the journey. A later acceleration brought the Toledo-Elkhart time, with diesel traction, down to 108 minutes, to improve the average speed to 74.1mph. Such times demanded speeds of well over 80mph for much of the distance, with a train which, even after the introduction of streamlined lightweight coaches, weighed well over 1,000 tons.

As to *Twentieth Century Limited* motive power: with the relatively light loads of the early years 4-4-0 locomotives (such as the famous No 999) were able to cope. As weight grew there was a progressive change to the 4-4-2 and 4-6-2 wheel arrangements and then to the highly capable Class J3 4-6-4, or Hudson class.

A Hudson in working order weighed 160¾ tons; with a twelve-wheel tender carrying nearly twenty-seven tons of coal and 14,000 gallons of water the weight was 300 tons. With the Hudsons the practice began of using the same locomotive unchanged between Harmon, where the changeover from electric haulage took place, and Chicago, a total distance of 925 miles. The water supply was replenished from time to time from track-troughs, and at two points en route coal was topped up from gantries spanning the line. There also, during a brief stop, the engines were given a quick service examination by attendant fitters.

But something bigger and even more imposing came with the arrival of the Niagara class 4-8-4s. To provide adequate supplies, these monsters needed a fourteen-wheel tender, with accommodation for 18,000 gallons of water and forty-one tons of coal (which nevertheless required replenishment en route). The tender weighed 188 tons fully loaded and engine and tender together totalled a little less than 400 tons.

Remarkable work was done by the Niagara 4-8-4s during their relatively short life, but as with all other American steam power they were doomed to give way to diesels, and actually did so in 1945, from which time 2,000hp Electro-motive diesel-electric locomotives in pairs took over the *Twentieth Century* duty. From that time onwards economies were achieved by a reduction in the cost of fuel and the abolition of the need to refuel or service the locomotives during the journey.

The glamour of the *Century* was not to be found only in its speed and long journeys. Every day at New York's Grand Central station a red carpet was rolled out along the entire length of the *Century*'s platform as a salute to its highly favoured passengers!

Great Railroads
UNION PACIFIC

T HE FIRST TRANSCONTINENTAL railroad across the United States of America was completed by the ceremonial driving in of a Golden Spike at Promontory Point, west of Ogden, Utah, on 10 May 1869. Much has been written of the original construction of that most important main line. It is sufficient to say here that today's Union Pacific Railroad route from Omaha,

Nebraska, or rather Council Bluffs, Iowa, on the east bank of the Missouri river, to Ogden (about 994 miles) is a very different property from the pioneer route of 1869.

With little doubt, Union Pacific is the most important of all the main lines linking the Middle West with the Pacific Coast, for the UP did not get nearer to Chicago than Omaha. For many years its

through expresses were handled to and from that Middle-West centre over 488 miles of the Chicago & North Western line, but in 1955 the traffic was handed over to the progressive Chicago, Milwaukee, St Paul & Pacific Railroad, whose route was of exactly the same length. In 1973 the Interstate Commerce Commission approved a merger of the bulk of the Rock Island system with UP, which

might eventually lead to UP's use of Rock Island tracks between Chicago and Omaha.

Over nearly the whole 990 miles of the main line from Omaha to Ogden, Utah, the Union Pacific has the unique distinction, for the USA, of double track throughout. At Julesburg, 363 miles from Omaha, a 197-mile branch diverges to the southwest to Denver, capital of Colorado. Next, at Granger, 844 miles, a 944-mile line branches north-west to Portland, Oregon. From Ogden another tentacle stretches south-westerly 821 miles across the desert country of Utah and Nevada finally to reach Los Angeles. A short section of the last-named line, across the Cajon pass from Barstow, is shared with the Atchison, Topeka & Santa Fe Railway. But what of San Francisco? Eventually the former Central Pacific Railroad, which in 1869 met the westward-advancing Union Pacific at Promontory, was absorbed by the Southern Pacific Railroad, and it is the Southern Pacific that takes over at Ogden from the Union Pacific for the 785-mile run to San Francisco.

Another distinction of the Union Pacific is that it reaches the second highest altitude of all the transcontinental lines. Climbing gradually westward from Omaha, after Cheyenne it faces the one in sixty-five ascent of Sherman hill, which takes it to a summit 8,013 feet above the sea. For the next 360 miles the line is never below 6,270 feet and it climbs finally to Aspen summit, 7,230 feet, before dropping down to Ogden. For tackling these gradients, the Union Pacific has always been noted for its motive power. In the days of steam,

Above: No 4021, one of Union Pacific's massive 'Big Boy' 4-8-8-4s, attacks Sherman Hill with eighty-two freight cars in September 1946. *R. H. Kindig*

Below: Union Pacific livery stands out on these two EMD 'Geep' diesels near Cheyenne, Wyoming, in 1960. *Blackhawk Films*

Overleaf: The first EMD 6,600hp eight-axle Type DDA40X diesel was delivered to Union Pacific in 1969 and the type became known as the 'Centennial' in honour of the Golden Spike ceremony at Promontory, Utah, in 1869. *Union Pacific Railroad*

development led to the giant 4-8-4s, 4-12-2s (a unique wheel formation for freight service), and 4-6-6-4 and 4-8-8-4 Challenger and Big Boy articulated types. In later years, as described earlier, the UP achieved distinction in another way, by introducing a fleet of powerful gas turbine-electric locomotives working freight over the 176 miles between Green River, Wyoming, and Ogden, including the negotiation of Aspen summit. Now, however, diesels are again in sole possession.

The flatter stretch of the main line, for 400 miles west from Omaha, was a speedway of considerable note. Over it in the 1950s and 1960s there ran a procession of streamlined trains – the *City of Los Angeles, City of San Francisco, City of Portland, City of Denver, Challenger* and others, with many station-to-station runs timed at 70mph and some up to 75mph. From Chicago to San Francisco and Los Angeles the mountains offered no restraint to speeds of 57.9mph and 56.8 mph over distances of 2,301 and 2,257 miles respectively; over the 1,048 miles between Chicago and Denver the *City of Denver* managed an average of 66.8 mph.

The original line of the Southern Pacific section of the 'Overland' route to San Francisco skirted the north shore of the Great Salt Lake, west of Salt Lake City, and included steep gradients and sharp curvature. Eventually, the Southern Pacific decided to cut straight across the lake, which it did by tipping rock and soil to provide twenty miles of embankments, and bridging the remainder by piling with thousands of long trees to form a trestle viaduct. The new line, thirty-one and a half miles in length and straight and level, cut forty-four and a half miles off the original route.

Union Pacific's 9,000 miles of route include many other main lines. Among the earliest of them was the Denver Pacific, a relatively short branch from the main line at Cheyenne to the burgeoning city of Denver, 106 miles away, and completed in 1870. Later, Denver was to have a more direct UP route to the east, joining the original transcontinental route at Julesburg, 197 miles from Denver, in the extreme north-east corner of Colorado. This was the route taken by the streamliner *City of Denver,* which competed with Burlington's *Denver Zephyr* for Chicago-Denver traffic. Another early component was the Kansas Pacific, a 640-mile route from Denver to Kansas City and thence east to St Louis over the Wabash Railway (now part of the Norfolk & Western). Over this route ran the streamliner *City of St Louis,* later called the *City of Kansas City.*

Subsequently, Union Pacific put out its own links to reach the Pacific coast. First came the Oregon Short Line, leaving the main transcontinental route at Granger, Wyoming, and then heading north-west through Pocatello (214 miles) and Hinkle (756 miles) to Portland (940 miles). From Portland, UP tracks head north a further 183 miles to Seattle, via Tacoma. Both Portland and Seattle are important ports, and also interchange points with other railroads serving the north-west Pacific area. Union Pacific reaches other important sources of traffic by major branch lines. From Pocaletto, the mines at Butte (263 miles) are served, as well as West Yellowstone, while from Hinkle the city of Spokane (191 miles) and Washington's agricultural area are reached, besides Yakima, centre of a fruit-growing area.

Last of UP's chief links is the Los Angeles & Salt Lake road, which brought UP service to Southern California. From Ogden, the route serves the Utah State capital of Salt Lake City, only thirty-six miles south of Ogden, before crossing the great deserts of Utah and Nevada as it runs south-west via Las Vegas to reach the Los Angeles area after crossing the spectacular Cajon pass. This 821-mile extension brought Union Pacific to tidal waters on its own tracks, and also gave access to the industries and major fruit and vegetable growing areas around Los Angeles.

Far left, top: A Union Pacific freight train paces automobiles on the Lincoln Highway near Cheyenne, Wyoming. Highway and railroad run close to each other for most of the way across Nebraska and eastern Wyoming. *Blackhawk Films*

Far left, centre: A Union Pacific steam 4-8-4 and a 6,600hp 'Centennial' diesel at Ogden for the UP Centennial ceremonies. *Union Pacific Railroad*

Far left, bottom, and left: Two views of Union Pacific's massive hump classification yard at North Platte, Nebraska. *Union Pacific Railroad*

Above left: The eastbound 'City of Francisco' en route for Chicago near Ragan, Wyoming, in pre-Amtrak days. *Union Pacific Railroad*

Great Railroads
SOUTHERN PACIFIC

SOUTHERN PACIFIC LINES extend for nearly 13,500 route miles, a figure which exceeds that of the Santa Fe only as a result of its recent acquisition of control of the Cotton Belt line – the St Louis-Southwestern Railway, in which Southern Pacific has had a majority holding since 1932. Southern Pacific Lines is the title used by the Southern Pacific Transportation Company for its railway operations; SPT Co also operates pipelines and highway freight services. SP is already well past its centenary, having had its origins in the Sacramento Valley Railroad, which ex-

tended twenty-one miles east from Sacramento, California, and was opened in 1855 to serve the gold camps in the foothills of the Sierra Nevada mountains.

The first important part of the Southern Pacific was the Central Pacific Railroad. Chartered originally only to build that portion of the first transcontinental railway within the State of California, Central Pacific built east from Sacramento, climbed the Sierra Nevada rising to the rim of the canyon of the American river, surmounted Donner pass, then crossed into Nevada, following the Humboldt river. It passed into Utah and finally met

the Union Pacific to the north of the Great Salt Lake at Promontory. The four main financial backers of the Central Pacific – Charles Crocker, Mark Hopkins, Collis P. Huntington and Leland Stanford – turned to building and acquiring other lines in California, and so built up the Southern Pacific which leased the Central Pacific in 1885.

The Southern Pacific forms part of two other transcontinental routes. The most southerly, the Sunset route, extends from New Orleans via El Paso, Tucson and Phoenix to Los Angeles, 2,033 miles. In 1894, SP inaugurated the *Sunset Limited*

over the route, and the train took fifty-eight hours to travel from New Orleans to Los Angeles. In contrast to the high altitudes of the other transcontinental lines, the Sunset route skirts the Salton Sea in Southern California, 202 feet *below* sea level. West of El Paso, the Sunset route is shared by trains of the Golden State route, which use the Southern Pacific line north-east out of El Paso to Tucumcari (331 miles) in north-east New Mexico, where an end-on junction is made with the Rock Island Lines from Chicago via Kansas City.

South of the San Francisco Bay area Southern Pacific has two quite separate

Far left: above: Southern Pacific's overnight 'Cascade' from Portland to San Francisco at Eugene, Oregon.
Southern Pacific

Far left, below: The 'Sunset Limited' crosses the Mississippi River at New Orleans in its 2,040-mile run to Los Angeles. *Ed Wotjas*

Below: A semi-streamlined 4-8-4 of Class GS-6 built by Lima in 1943 for Southern Pacific freight service. *Blackhawk Films*

Right: Southern Pacific's 'Shasta Daylight' headed by an Alco passenger diesel unit round the foot of Mount Shasta in the summer of 1962. *Southern Pacific*

routes to Los Angeles. From the city itself, the coast route goes south via San Jose (forty-seven miles), to which point commuter service is operated, over Paso Robles and then via San Luis Obispo and Santa Barbara to Los Angeles, 470 miles. For over a hundred miles, the line is within sight of the Pacific ocean. The other route starts from Oakland, runs across the bay from San Francisco, and proceeds east, skirting San Pablo Bay and Suisun Bay before turning south into the San Joaquin valley, via Merced and Fresno to Bakersfield (313 miles). There, the easy gadients end and the line climbs to the summit loop built around a cone-shaped hill, to gain height in the Tehachapi mountains (3,967 feet) before crossing the western end of the Mojave Desert, and descending to Los Angeles (479 miles). The last few miles from Burbank are shared with the coastal route.

North from San Francisco, or rather Oakland, Southern Pacific has its Shasta route (parallel to the coast, but well inland) which takes it through the Redwood forests of Northern California and Oregon to Portland; a road of 712 miles. The Shasta route included an important alternative route to the east of the original line over Grants Pass – the Cascade line via Klamath Falls, completed in 1927. The new line is about twenty-five miles shorter than the old Siskiyou line.

Across the Golden Gate and north from Marin county up the Northern Californian coast is another track of the Southern Pacific: the Northwestern Pacific Railroad. It is a combination of a number of small companies, some of which operated commuter services in the bay area, with ferry links to San Francisco, until the opening of the Golden Gate bridge killed the traffic. The SP gained control of the

NWP in 1929, and maintained passenger service over the northern end of the line, between Willits and Eureka, until the formation of Amtrak in May 1971. Latterly, the service was run only twice weekly, worked by a solitary railcar, but it provided access to the isolated Eel River valley.

The Southern Pacific had a number of other rail interests, including some electrically operated lines. Two branch lines south-west of Portland were electrified in 1912-14, but electric services there ceased in 1929. In the San Francisco Bay area, some of the Northwestern Pacific commuter lines were electrified in 1903, and discontinued in 1941; while in the east bay area, around Oakland, several lines electrified in 1911-12 were also abandoned in 1941. Much the largest of the electrified systems was the Pacific Electric Railway, extending over 520 miles of route. The SP gained control in

1911, by which time the PER was already changing from an interurban to a suburban operation, as the area it served rapidly developed. Its value to SP was largely as a freight feeder from all over the greater Los Angeles area. Cut-backs in PER passenger service began before the Second World War. Very heavy wartime traffic stemmed the decline, but contraction continued after the war, until the last passenger service closed in 1963.

Perhaps the early abandonment of local passenger traffic was a portent of the future of long-distance trains, for by the early nineteen-sixties, SP's disenchantment with passengers had become very evident; and that despite its fleet of streamlined named trains – the Coast and Valley Daylights, the Shasta, the Cascade and others – on which standards had once been very high. Service was deliberately downgraded; restaurant- and sleeping-cars were withdrawn even from trains

with journeys extending over two nights. The wanton behaviour eventually attracted official notice and permission for further discontinuances was refused by the regulatory bodies on the ground that substantial traffic had been deliberately discouraged by the deterioration of standards.

Today Amtrak provides service over four different Southern Pacific routes. The *Coast Starlight* is operated daily between Los Angeles, Oakland (for San Francisco and via San Jose) and Seattle. Thrice-weekly service is offered on the other routes – the *Southern Crescent* and *Sunset Limited* between Los Angeles, New Orleans and Atlanta, the *Coast Starlight* between Portland and Oakland, and the *San Francisco Zephyr* between Oakland and Chicago which operates daily. In the spring of 1974 Amtrak added a daily service, the *San Joaquin*, up the valley of the same name from Oakland to Bakers-

field; it takes the SP waterside route along Carquinez Strait out of Oakland to Port Chicago, thirty-six miles; but from there onward the train is in Sante Fe territory.

Above left: Amtrak's 'Coast Daylight' hugs the Californian coast between Santa Barbara and San Luis Obispo. *Amtrak*

Top: A Southern Pacific TOFC train of piggybacked highway trailers rounds the horseshoe curve near San Luis Obispo, helped by two diesel units cut in near the rear of the train. *Southern Pacific RR*

Above: Another SP piggyback train, headed by two EMD SD45 diesels, below the Rockies. *Southern Pacific RR*

Great Railroads
SANTA FE

THE ATCHISON, TOPEKA & SANTA FE Railway had its beginnings in the State of Kansas, where it was granted a charter to build the Colorado State line in 1859. Only with the spur of a substantial grant of land – with a time limit of ten years – did construction get under way in 1868. Starting from the state capital, Topeka, (sixty-six miles west of Kansas City), Dodge City became end-of-line in 1871, and the Colorado State line was reached in 1872. The Atchison & Topeka, as the line was then known, played a major part in the settlement of Kansas, and its colonization agents sought potential farmers in the Menonites, a Russian religious sect, among others.

Although the town of Santa Fe, capital of New Mexico, became the next goal, the main line bypassed it, as construction proceeded across South-east Colorado to Albuquerque, and the capital was served by a short branch line from Lamy. To reach Albuquerque, the Raton Pass, near the New Mexico-Colorado State line, had to be surmounted. The physical problems there, however, were second to those presented by the young and expanding Denver & Rio Grande Railroad, which at that period was still moving south from Denver; later, it was to head west, into the Rockies.

Battles, both physical and legal, ensued; the Sante Fe won and its first train surmounted Raton at the end of 1878. With its title extended to Atchison, Topeka & Santa Fe, the railway looked even farther west. The Southern Pacific, however, considered New Mexico to be its own territory, and opposed the ex-

pansion. The Sante Fe parried by obtaining an interest in a charter owned by the St Louis and San Francisco Railroad. Further legal suits ensued, but finally the Santa Fe was able to build through to the Pacific coast, and complete its line to Los Angeles in 1887.

At its eastern end, acquisitions and new construction brought the Santa Fe to Chicago. Included there was the

Left, above: Two 2-10-2s and a 4-8-2 of Santa Fe climbing Raton Pass in New Mexico with a mail train in March 1946. *R. H. Kindig*

Left, below: Santa Fe 2-10-4 No 5017, westbound, crosses the plains of New Mexico near Tejon in October 1947. *R. H. Kindig*

Above, right: Five EMD GP35 diesels head a Santa Fe unit coal train for the Kaiser steel plant at Fontana, California, near Fenner. *Santa Fe Railway*

Right: A triple-diesel-headed Santa Fe freight crossing the Colorado River near Needles. *J. F. Curto*

Below: Santa Fe's 'San Francisco Chief' ready to leave Richmond, California, in May 1968, with its two-storey Hi-Level cars behind the leading mail/baggage car. *C. V. Ehrke*

Chicago & St Louis Railroad, whose line of ninety miles from Chicago to Streator, Illinois, provided the entry link to the big city. The Santa Fe stretched 2,224 miles from Chicago to Los Angeles. Later construction brought the Santa Fe to San Francisco Bay, at Oakland. From Barstow, the line ran to Bakersfield and thence down the San Joaquin Valley via Stockton and Richmond, to a terminal at Oakland, 454 miles from Barstow.

From Chicago to Los Angeles, the main line today is double track throughout, except where alternative routes are available between Newton, Kansas, and the Albuquerque area, and between Los Angeles and San Bernardino, California. Santa Fe faces the most difficult conditions of all the transcontinental routes, with four high summits in succession over the Continental and Arizona Divides. Raton Pass comes first (7,573 feet), with an approach in part as steep as one in twenty-eight; then Glorieta (7,437 feet); Campbell Pass (7,247 feet); and Flagstaff (7,310 feet); after which comes the tremendous drop to Needles, in the Colorado River Valley, at 483 feet alti-

Top: Another Santa Fe unit coal train near Flagstaff, Arizona. *Santa Fe Railway*

Right: Santa Fe piggyback yard at Corwith, Chicago. *Santa Fe Railway*

Below: One of three mobile cranes used for road-rail transfers of containers and highway trailers at Corwith yard. *Santa Fe Railway*

tude. But that is not all, for before the line reaches Los Angeles there is the Cajon Pass to be tackled, with a 3,822 feet summit. The alternative main line via Amarillo, Texas, forty-six miles longer, has a summit level of only 6,470 feet at Mountainair. Most passenger trains used the old main line via La Junta, which initially had been built to Pueblo, Colorado, before the extensions into New Mexico had left Pueblo on a sixty-four-mile-long branch from La Junta. Pueblo gave connections to the Colorado mining areas, and eventually by joint trackage and running agreements to Denver. Other western extensions took the Santa Fe to San Diego and to El Paso: two points with Mexican connections.

Apart from its coverage in the far south-west, the Santa Fe also served much of Texas, and reached the Gulf of Mexico. From Newton, Kansas, on the main line, a 200-mile-long extension leads to Oklahoma City, and from there (over the rails of the subsidiary Gulf, Colorado & Santa Fe Railway) Fort Worth, Dallas, Houston and the port of Galveston are reached. Western Texas is served by another subsidiary, the Panhandle and Santa Fe Railway. Altogether, the Santa Fe system covers 13,000 miles of route. Until the recent creation of the Penn Central and Burlington Northern, it was the longest rail system in the USA. Serving areas which are economically still expanding, and with a high proportion of long-haul and high-rated traffic, the Santa Fe is a prosperous and well-kept railway.

In the middle nineteen-fifties, freight revenue outstripped that from passengers in the ratio of twelve to one, but a procession of distinguished trains still used the Santa Fe main line daily – the all-Pullman extra-fare *Super-Chief*, the *Chief*, the *El Capitan* (conveying the equivalent of second-class passengers in reclining chairs, and made up latterly entirely of hi-level cars), and the *San Francisco Chief.* Across the prairies very high speeds were run; all four trains were booked over the 127.2 miles from Gallup to Winslow in 102 minutes at 74.8mph, and there were other start-to-stop bookings exceeding 80mph. Over a line with such formidable gradients it was no mean achievement for the *Super-Chief* and the *El Capitan* both to cover the 2,226 miles between Chicago and Los Angeles under forty hours at an average speed of 56mph. The fleet name of *Chief* had its origin in a train advertised as 'The Chief – extra fast, extra fine, and extra fare', which entered service towards the

Top: A Santa Fe EMD 2,300hp GP39-2 diesel road switcher. *Santa Fe Railway*

Centre: A six-diesel combination attacks the steep Cajon Pass in California, heading east with freight from the West Coast. *Santa Fe Railway*

Left: Part of Santa Fe's automated classification yard at Kansas City. *Santa Fe Railway*

end of 1926 on the Chicago-Los Angeles route. Before that, the *Santa Fe De Luxe* and the *California Limited,* both crack trains, had been companions on the run.

Closely associated with passenger service on the Santa Fe from as early as 1876 was 'Fred Harvey' service. Harvey was a Scot who built up a chain of railway station restaurants on Santa Fe lines, before the days of dining-cars. He set high standards at a time when train meal stops were a prime subject for jokes. The Harvey Houses made a name for themselves, and expanded to become a big hotel group; for a time Harvey was also a dining-car contractor.

History was made in 1937 when the Santa Fe placed in service the first diesel-powered all-first-class streamliner in the USA. The *Super-Chief* was a beautifully appointed train, built by Budd, and it ran from Chicago to Los Angeles in under forty hours. In 1938, it was joined by a

second similar train, built by Pullman-Standard. Dome-cars and more new equipment were added after the war and, in 1956, the fast all-coach (second-class) economy train, the *El Capitan,* was equipped with so-called high-level coaches. Other crack trains of the Santa Fe included the *Texas Chief* and the *Kansas Cityan.*

Amtrak still maintains a Chicago-Los Angeles service over Santa Fe tracks. Santa Fe was slow to give up the long-haul passenger business, for it had invested in new equipment for its services quite recently and was more reluctant than its neighbours to trim its passenger timetable before the creation of Amtrak. Nor was it happy to hand over its highly respected train names to Amtrak. Eventually, reluctant permission was given to Amtrak to perpetuate the *Chief, Super-Chief, El Capitan* and *Texas Chief* titles, but Santa Fe reserved the right to

rescind the authority should Amtrak downgrade the services to the extent that they 'no longer reflect credit on Santa Fe'. In the spring of 1974 Santa Fe exercised that right. In their view Amtrak was no longer providing sufficient accommodation to avoid serious overcrowding of diner and lounge facilities which, said Santa Fe President John S. Reed, 'determine the entire character and comfort of a long-distance train trip'.

So the daily Chicago-Kansas City-Los Angeles service is now the *Southwest Limited* and the daily Chicago-Houston train the *Lone Star.* On the West Coast, the four-times-daily *San Diegan* service between Los Angeles and San Diego has been re-equipped with Amtrak's latest Amfleet equipment, which generated a substantial upswing in patronage at the start of 1977. Santa Fe also has the main operational responsibility for the Oakland-Bakersfield San Joaquin service.

Amtrak has further hopes of starting a Kansas City-Denver service, but this is one of several developments hinging on an improvement of its shaky budget.

Below: Two cowl-bodied FP45 3,600 diesels, specially styled by EMD for Santa Fe passenger haulage, at Chicago's Dearborn station. *J. K. Hayward*

Right: Exterior of a double-deck lounge car in the Hi-Level stock built for Santa Fe's 'El Capitan'. *Cecil J. Allen Collection*

Right, centre: Inside the upper deck of a Hi-Level lounge. *Cecil J. Allen Collection*

Right, bottom: Lower-deck cocktail bar of a Hi-Level lounge car. *Cecil J. Allen Collection*

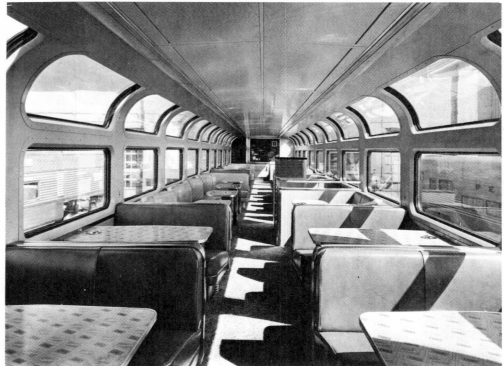

Great Railroads
EXIT PENN-CENTRAL: ENTER CONRAIL

ON 1 FEBRUARY 1968, after a struggle of ten years and final settlement at the US Supreme Court, the New York Central and Pennsylvania Railroads merged officially as the Pennsylvania–New York Central Transportation Co: otherwise, Penn-Central, or PC for short. The most unlikely combination in all North American railroading had been arranged.

The New York Central and Pennsylvania had always seemed to take such opposite courses that a union between the two was thought to be wildly improbable. Then there came the decrease in traffic and increase in costs after the Second World War that caused many railways to look upon long-standing and hated rivals as new-found friends and saviours.

Movement towards merger began with the Louisville & Nashville Railroad in 1955. During the next decade more than fifty proposals for merger were submitted to the Interstate Commerce Commission (the United States Federal regulatory body for transport). Many such mergers concerned only small operators, but there were several alliances between major railroads. Among them were the Norfolk & Western's take-over of the Virginian, and the Norfolk & Western's absorption of the Nickel Plate, Wabash and some

smaller systems; the merger of the Erie and Delaware, Lackawanna & Western as the Erie—Lackawanna; and the Chesapeake & Ohio take-over of the Baltimore & Ohio. Such were some of the bigger unions that provided precedents for the creation of Penn-Central.

The New York Central was itself the result of the consolidation in 1853 of a number of short lines to form a through route from the capital of New York State, Albany, to Buffalo. Then there appeared Commodore Cornelius Vanderbilt, flushed at the age of sixty-eight with a fortune of more than $11,000,000 amassed from his steamboat enterprises before the Civil War. After gaining control of the New York Central, and having acquired routes from Albany into New York City, and a route from Buffalo along the south shore of Lake Erie to Chicago via Cleveland and Toledo, Vanderbilt had by 1869 established the main artery of New York Central's network. Thereafter the system was expanded by stages to embrace Detroit, Cincinnati, Columbus, Indianapolis and St Louis, and Boston.

The line to Boston opened up a valuable outlet for New England freight, via the Boston & Albany, which was leased to the New York Central. NYC's other important subsidiary was the Pittsburgh & Lake Erie, which was significant out of

all proportion to its size because of its access to the steel industry and coal mines in and around Pittsburgh. NYC also secured a gateway to Canada by connection at Massena, in the north of New York State, with the Grand Trunk Western (which became a subsidiary of Canadian National), and a link that enabled a through service between New York and Montreal.

Like NYC, Pennsylvania created a substantial network in the States of New York, Indiana, Illinois, Michigan and Ohio. The line was incorporated in 1846 by a group of Philadelphia businessmen who were worried that the superior communications with the west from ports to the north and south of them would make Philadelphia a backwater. Their concern was not lessened by the fact that at that time Philadelphia was the biggest and most important city in the United States.

Pennsylvania's first objective was Chicago and the Mississippi. In contrast to NYC's gentle line of route, Pennsylvania drove through the Allegheny Mountains on some severe gradients — among them the spectacular Horseshoe

Below: EMD diesels at Cleveland with NYC's New York-Chicago 'Iroquois' in September 1963. *W. E. Zullig.*

Left: Steam and diesel power side by side in East Altoona yard of the Pennsylvania RR in August 1952. *J. M. Jarvis*

Below: Vintage suburban electric stock of the Pennsylvania RR at Washington Union station in February 1972. *B. W. Mouat*

Bottom: Three EMD F-Type diesels wind a Pennsylvania freight round the Horseshoe Curve at Altoona. *J. M. Jarvis*

Curve that attracted so many photographers in times of steam. Pittsburgh was reached late in 1852, while other railroads were already building a system from Pittsburgh to Chicago that was consolidated in 1856 as the Pittsburgh, Fort Wayne and Chicago. Two years later the whole route to Chicago was open, and soon afterwards Pennsylvania took it over.

Although Pennsylvania and New York Central crowded each other west of Pittsburgh, NYC had much less mileage than Pennsylvania in Pennsylvania itself and in New Jersey. Here was the other principal Pennsylvania trunk route – from Philadelphia to Baltimore and Washington – which, with the New York-Philadelphia line, constitutes half of today's North-East Corridor railroad. It was still in Pennsylvania's hands in the 1960s when the Government-sponsored high-speed demonstration service was set up with the 125 mph Metroliner electric sets. By the time of the Metroliners' launch in January 1969, however, the Penn-Central merger had taken place.

Another Pennsylvania service ran to Atlantic City. In the Camden-Atlantic City-Cape May area Pennsylvania and the Reading Railroad ran parallel and overlapped each other. After the slump of the 1930s the two systems agreed to stop wasteful competition. Their routes were put under a joint management (not a common event in United States railroading) and entitled the Pennsylvania-Reading Seashore Lines.

New York Central's imposing Grand Central station in New York City, with its two levels of underground platforms and extensive commuter services, was an early twentieth-century creation that required heavy investment. No steam locomotives ran into the station. The line was electrified to Harmon, thirty-three miles out, on the third-rail direct current system, and all inter-city expresses had to call there to change their style of power. In more recent times self-contained train-sets like the Rohr-built, French-style Turboliners on the New York-Montreal *Adirondack* service have been fitted with pick-up shoes and supplementary low-power electric traction motors so that they can switch from their main power to straight electric power for the run into and out of Grand Central.

Grand Central was also the New York terminal for all suburban and most inter-city services of the New York, New Haven & Hartford Railroad, though New Haven trains making connections for points to the south and west of New York took the spectacular Hell Gate Bridge high-level route into Pennsylvania's Manhattan station. New Haven intended to electrify its route all the way to Boston, but funds gave out after the overhead wires had been installed over the seventy-two miles from New York to Haven, and over the New Canaan and Danbury branches. The New Haven's electrification was at 11,000V alternating current, so its locomotives could not work into and out of Grand Central unless they were also fitted to work off the NYC third-rail system.

The early twentieth century had arrived before Pennsylvania advanced into Manhattan from its ferry-served terminal on the opposite side of the water in Jersey

City. A tunnel under the Hudson River led to a new station on a twenty-eight acre site in mid-town New York. The line continued in another tunnel under the East River to Long Island and to a connection with the Hell Gate Bridge route and the New Haven road which opened up a through route from the south to Boston. In 1900 Pennsylvania had taken over the Long Island Railroad – the tight-knit system that handles about a quarter of all United States commuter business – and the Long Island trains also were run into the new Penn station, which was far more conveniently located than the former Long Island terminals.

After electrifying its tunnel lines to a third-rail direct current system, Pennsylvania switched to 11,000V 25-cycle alternating current which by the late 1930s had extended all the way to Washington and as far as Harrisburg on the main route to Pittsburgh and the Midwest. Thus New Haven and Pennsylvania were electrified to the same system, and when the two lines were fused after New Haven's financial crash Pennsylvania's much-loved and elegant electric locomotives of the 1930s could work unchanged through New York between the south and New Haven. The whole Washington-New York-Boston route is now being re-electrified to the modern 25kV 60-cycle alternating current system.

The New York Central and Pennsylvania were regarded as leading examples of the North American railroad system by railway people within and outside the United States – indeed, Pennsylvania proudly claimed to be the 'Standard Railroad of the World'. Rivalry between the two lines was intense, especially in the long-haul passenger traffic between New York and Chicago. NYC's 960-mile route was longer but much easier. The Pennsylvania route measured only 908 miles, but west of Philadelphia its gradients were tough.

On the roads the rivalry was led by two world-famous trains – *Twentieth Century Limited* of New York Central, and Pennsylvania's *Broadway Limited.* Both trains were given the latest machinery and the most luxurious cars that designers and

builders had to offer. Between the turn of the century and the beginning of the Second World War both trains had reduced the running time for the journey between New York and Chicago from twenty-eight to sixteen hours.

Even before the war passenger trains in the United States were costing more to run than they earned. In 1937, for dining-cars alone, Pennsylvania was losing $1,000,000 over the year on train meals with menus that, respectable as they were, fell far short of the expansive Chicago & North Western dinner of 1887 which offered a choice of thirteen entrées, six varieties of game and twenty-five desserts for only seventy-five cents. The war induced so much traffic back to the railways that passenger business recovered and became profitable, but only for the time being.

After the war the railroads invested vast sums of money in new equipment and policies designed to hold their position against other forms of transport. NYC, for example, laid out $250,000,000 on passenger cars alone between 1945 and 1958; and in 1952 Pennsylvania paid $3,250,000 for eighteen cars for the train-set of the *New Congressional* on the New York-Washington route. However, such investment was in vain. For, whereas in 1949 the railways had eighty

Top: In Penn-Central livery, an EMD E-Type unit heads the lightweight 'Admiral' out of Chicago in July 1970. *V. Goldberg*

Above: The New York that was: an impression of the Pennsylvania station at the turn of the century. *V. Goldberg*

Right, above: A General Electric Type E60CP electric locomotive working under Pennsylvania catenary for Amtrak is seen heading a train of Amfleet cars in the North-East Corridor. *Amtrak*

Right, below: New York's Grand Central station as it looked before it was submerged under high-rise building. *V. Goldberg*

per cent of the total air-rail passenger miles travelled in the USA, by 1960 their share had fallen to thirty-nine per cent, and by 1968 to as little as twelve per cent. At the same time, other passengers were being lost to inter-city buses and private motoring. In 1946 the railroads made a net loss on their passenger services of $139,000,000; in 1953 the loss was $704,000,000. For the largest passenger-carrying railroads the effects of competition were appalling.

Nor was railroad freight traffic in much better shape. Rail held on pretty well to the bulk freight which it was inherently suited to handle, such as coal, grain and ore, but other merchandise went steadily

Grand Central Terminal Station, New York City.

to the trucking industry. With both passenger and freight revenue declining, railroads, unable to reduce their fixed assets, were compelled to trim their running costs and investment wherever they could. One area where savings could be made was in track maintenance. By the mid-1970s, overdue track maintenance work was estimated at a massive $6-7,500,000,000.

Eastern railroads were in far the worst state. The first tremor of the approaching calamity came in 1961 when the New Haven line became bankrupt. New York Central and Pennsylvania were already talking about merger and rationalization as the only way out of their deepening financial problems. The proposal to merge was put formally to the Interstate Commerce Commission in 1962. However, so apprehensive was the reaction of other railroads and of the NYC-Pennsylvania customers to the great network that was envisaged, and so complicated were side-issues concerning neighbouring railroads, that the proposal had to face a seemingly interminable series of discussions, hearings, petitions and judicial proceedings before the Supreme Court finally gave approval in 1968.

Until later mergers created the Burlington Northern, Penn-Central was by far the country's biggest railroad in route-

mileage (19,286) and other assets and in revenue. At the time of the merger, Penn-Central disposed of 4,202 locomotives, 4,937 passenger cars (including self-propelled stock) and 194,656 freight cars valued at more than $4,000,000,000.

The merger never achieved the scale of economies that had been expected. The NYC and Pennsylvania electronic data transmission systems proved to be incompatible and led to such farcical muddles as freight cars being sent to a former NYC yard when they were expected at an ex-Pennsylvania yard, and vice versa. Savings on labour were slight because of a pre-merger agreement that only death or normal retirement would cause reductions in staff. Above all, the rivalries and jealousies of the original companies intensified, rather than abated, to the point of refusal to collaborate or compromise on differences of policy at managerial level.

Nowhere were the NYC-Pennsylvania feuds more conspicuous than at the very top. There, neither Alfred E. Perlman (NYC's former president and a career railwayman) nor Stuart Saunders (a Harvard lawyer who had been chairman and chief executive of Pennsylvania) seemingly troubled to hide their failure to come to an agreeable working partnership.

At Saunders' instigation, and to Perlman's disgust, Penn-Central funds were ploughed into diversification, especially real estate, rather than into developing the railroad. Although, at great cost, Penn-Central was operating no less than three-quarters of the country's remaining passenger services, no attempt was made to effect sensible economies in the way that Perlman urged. Staffing costs remained much too high and there was the further burden of the bankrupt New Haven which Penn-Central had been compelled to take over as part of the terms of the merger.

At the same time, the country's economy was contracting and inflation was rampant. Not only were railroad revenues falling while costs increased, but Penn-Central's huge involvement in real estate failed to produce the hoped for return. Penn-Central resorted to borrowing heavily just to pay its wages until, in the spring of 1970, the bankers, now wary, refused further support. Congress declined the idea of a guaranteed Federal loan, and in June 1970 Penn-Central had no choice but to file a petition of bankruptcy.

By the time Congress could tackle the problem six more eastern railroads, responsible for some 17,000 miles of track, were also insolvent — Ann Arbor, Boston & Maine, Erie-Lackawanna, Lehigh Valley, Central of New Jersey, and Reading. There was a serious threat of complete closure of the railways in the eastern States, and an urgent and general solution of the crisis was imperative.

A number of schemes were put forward and from them Congress adopted, and President Nixon signed, the Rail Reorganization Act of 1973, which set up the Consolidated Rail Corporation supported by $2,000,000,000 of Government funds. This was to provide the eastern part of the country with a 'financially self-sustaining rail service'. The United States Railway Association, representative of the government, railroad management, trade unions and shippers, was created to plan the new organization and a system for approval. USRA was recommended to consider reduction and rationalization of the eastern rail network as a means of achieving profitability for the new corporation, but it was also instructed to preserve the existing patterns of service and to keep loss of employment among staff to the minimum. Other commitments included the establishment of a high-speed passenger service in the Washington-New York-Boston corridor, and otherwise to collaborate with Amtrak.

In 1974 USRA produced a preliminary plan which advocated elimination of some 5,700 miles of light-density and secondary track, unless local interests would subsidize their retention. To allay fears that the corporation might become monopolistic in its attitudes, USRA also suggested selling some 2,000 miles of track to the Chesapeake & Ohio, and Southern, and thereby extending those roads into the corporation's territory. The final plan of 1975 was changed only in detail and became the basis of the Rail Revitalization & Reform Act – popularly known as the '4R Act' – of 1975.

The 4R Act in its provisions had to tread a delicate path around outright nationalization, which would have been anathema to American opinion already aghast at the huge sums of money being poured into Amtrak. The new corporation, now generally known as Conrail, was made a 'quango' – a quasi-non-governmental organization. It was established as a private enterprise founded on share capital, but the Government took up debentures and preferred stock to provide the $2,100,000,000 needed to start Conrail operating.

The cost of the 4R Act to the Government reached about $6,000,000,000 in all, as the remedies for several other railway problems were gathered into the legislation. Most importantly, the Act provided for Amtrak to buy the North-East Corridor route from Washington to New York and Boston lock, stock and barrel, and to take over its rehabilitation for high-speed passenger service – this is described in the chapter 'Has Amtrak Reborn the Passenger Train?'.

The 4R Act did not have an easy passage. Congress behaved irresolutely and President Ford threatened a veto, which delayed progress and took the trustees of the bankrupt railroads that were to form Conrail unawares. They had been running down stocks in expectation of an early Conrail take-over and were reduced to their last reserves of such essential items as lubricating oil. Chesapeake & Ohio and Southern, unable to come to terms with the staff whom they would take over with the track offered to them, chose not to take up their options. Some of that track was later taken over by Delaware & Hudson, but even so Conrail started 2,000 miles larger than was originally intended (which, in consequence, put the corporation in a better competitive position). Finally, the trustees, shareholders and creditors of the bankrupt Penn-Central were furious at the valuation of $471,000,000,000 put by USRA on the 15,781 miles of track, 140,000 freight cars and 3,800 locomotives of their railroad that Conrail absorbed. Worse still, payment was to be made in Conrail stock, which would not yield a dividend for a decade at least.

Nevertheless, Conrail – which, like its Pennsylvania predecessor, is based on Philadelphia – became operational on 1 April 1976. It started life with a 17,000-route-mile network touching sixteen American States and two Canadian provinces, and 4,816 locomotives and 162,000 freight cars.

Since then progress has been undoubted. Consolidation of seven railroads under one management has removed a lot of wasteful competition on parallel routes. Loss-making commuter and lightly-loaded branch-line services have either been eliminated or are now a charge to another authority. And the first results of a massive programme of track rehabilitation, combined in some cases with the ending of remarshalling at former systems' borders, have led to some substantial cuts in freight transit times.

Many critics fear that Conrail is an extravagant time-buying expedient. They doubt whether the corporation will ever be able to trim either its staff or its system to a size that will reduce unit costs to the level of its budget, especially in view of still declining traffic.

The industrial base in the north-east is contracting steadily. Trucking competition, backed by powerful politicians and lobbyists in Conrail territory, will intensify with the completion of the inter-state highway system; and one of the eastern railroads' key freights, the movement of coal to generating stations, has been much reduced by the development of nuclear plants.

Perhaps Washington will yet have to look at the Penn-Central trustees' post-bankruptcy proposal to cut away half of the network and concentrate on the core that moves nearly ninety per cent of the railroad's traffic – a plan that was derided at the time by every State politician, community and shipper in Penn-Central country.

Below: A Pennsylvania Class K4s storms out of Fort Wayne on a December day in 1947. *Cecil J. Allen Collection*

THE BIGGEST US RAILROAD: BURLINGTON NORTHERN

BURLINGTON NORTHERN RAILROAD is a newcomer to the American railway scene. It dates only from 2 March 1970, when three major railways, and some other lines, were merged. The railways involved were the Chicago, Burlington & Quincy Railroad (Burlington Route – 8,500 miles), the Great Northern Railway (the route of the *Empire Builder* – 8,260 miles) and the Northern Pacific Railway ('Main Street of the North-West' – 6,780 miles). Also included were the Spokane, Portland & Seattle Railway – 950 miles, and the Pacific Coast Railroad – 32 miles.

The merger had been proposed more than once over the years and was finally approved only after prolonged enquiry by the Interstate Commerce Commission. For many years, however, there had been interlinking ownership between the various companies involved. The Great Northern and North Pacific owned jointly the Chicago, Burlington & Quincy, although the latter was larger than either of its parents. The GN and NP also owned jointly the Spokane, Portland & Seattle, which was geographically quite separate from the CB & Q. The CB & Q and the SP & S were also operated quite separately, and had their own managements.

With just on 23,000 miles of route and 33,900 track miles, Burlington Northern is second only to Canadian National Railways in size of system in North America, with Conrail a much smaller third.

Each of the three major components of Burlington Northern included numerous short, local, or bigger constituents, but the first to become a major system was the Northern Pacific. After the choice for the first transcontinental railroad fell to the central route, followed by the Union Pacific and Central Pacific to San Francisco, for which a charter was granted in 1862, pressure continued for the alternative route to be built. A further charter was granted in 1864, in the midst of the American Civil War, but construction of the Northern Pacific route, from both ends, began only in 1870. The eastern end started at Carlton, near Duluth, Minnesota, and the western end started, northwards initially, from the Columbia River, near Portland, Oregon. Bismarck, North Dakota, and Tacoma, Washington, had been reached from east and west respectively when a national financial crisis caused suspension of construction in 1873. Work resumed in 1879, and the transcontinental route of the Northern Pacific of 2,260 miles was finally completed in 1883. New construction and acquisition brought the Northern Pacific route mileage to about 6,780 at the time of the Burlington Northern marger. The main line, which is still largely (and unusually) signalled by semaphores, runs from the Twin Cities of St Paul – Minneapolis via Fargo, Bismarck, Mandon and Billings to Butte. At Butte is one of the world's largest openpit copper mines, served by the Butte, Anaconda & Pacific Railway, which until recently had electric traction. In the same area there is an alternative more northerly loop of the Northern Pacific serving Helena, the State capital of Montana. The two routes rejoin at Garrison, Montana, and the main line continues west to Spokane, Washington. A south-westerly course takes the route on to Pasco, Washington, through much of Washington State's fertile country, and so to the Puget Sound at Tacoma. From there tracks fork north to Seattle and south to Portland.

The Northern Pacific had several im-

Below: A Great Northern oil-burning Class R-2 2-8-8-2 and a heavy westbound freight in North Dakota, July 1953. *W. H. N. Rossiter*

Bottom: Bound for Portland and Seattle via the Northern Pacific, the 'North Coast Limited' at Naperville behind Burlington diesels. *Blackhawk Films*

portant secondary routes. From the Twin Cities, a line led up to the two lakehead ports, Duluth and Superior, which also had a direct route to the west via Brainerd to link with the main transcontinental route at Staples. A little to the west of Staples, and still in Minnesota, the Northern Pacific had a route via Grand Forks to Winnipeg, in Canada. North Dakota was served by a number of branch-lines. In Montana, a huge State ('Big Sky Country') which takes a whole day to cross (the rail mileage is about 760), Livingston is the gateway to the Yellowstone National Park. Westward from there, the main line follows a scenic route through the Big Belt and Bitter Root ranges of the Rocky Mountains. Much of the route west follows the trail of the Lewis and Clark expedition of 1804, particularly up the Yellowstone River in Montana.

The NP's 'herald', or crest, was unusual. An annular ring containing the words Northern Pacific surrounded a monad — a Chinese mystical symbol formed by a circle split into two equal parts by an S-shaped line. One half was black, the other red. The symbol appears to date from the inauguration of NP's crack train, the *North Coast Limited*, in 1900. The eight-car train had electric lighting and represented the peak of wooden carriage construction.

The *North Coast Limited* required six sets of equipment to maintain service and some new stock was added in 1909 and 1930, but the first large delivery of streamlined cars did not occur until 1947-48. In 1954 twenty dome-cars, both coaches (second-class) and sleepers, were acquired, to be followed by buffet-lounge cars in 1955 and six new diners in 1958. Finally, in 1959 slumber coaches (each named after a Scottish loch) were added, to make economy-class sleeping-accommodation available. The various additions to stock during the 1950s permitted the second-line transcontinental train, the *Mainstreeter*, to be

re-equipped, although latterly this train was formed of only five or six cars.

Northern Pacific passenger services were almost entirely dropped when the government-financed organization Amtrak took over responsibility, but political pressures soon brought back service over the NP main line, three days a week, on a 'trial' basis.

The Great Northern Railway had its beginnings in the St Paul & Pacific Railway, which had become moribund, after starting to build track north-westward out of St Paul. A young Ontario-born man, James Jerome Hill, moved to the west in 1856, intent on trading with the Orient. Instead, he became involved in river transport on the Mississippi, and later gained control of the St Paul & Pacific. He extended the line up to the Canadian border at Pembina, to which point the Canadian Pacific built a link south from Winnipeg. Until 1883, Hill was also associated with the Canadian Pacific Railway.

The St Paul-Winnipeg link prospered, and Hill resolved to extend westward to the Pacific Ocean. The new line followed a route between the Canadian border and the line of the Northern Pacific and was well engineered. The title Great Northern was adopted in 1890. In 1893, the line reached the Puget Sound at Everett, Washington, thirty-three miles north of Seattle. The route reached a summit of 5,213 feet above sea-level, twelve miles west of Glacier Park station, and only fifty-five miles of route were higher than 4,000 feet, an important consideration when winter snows are considered.

The Great Northern crossing of the Cascade Mountains was greatly improved in 1929 when the original Cascade tunnel (two and two-thirds miles) was replaced with one seven and three-quarters miles long. The new tunnel formed part of a seventy-three-mile electrification at 11,500-volt twenty-five-cycle alternating current, which replaced an earlier three-phase system. The later

Above left: A Burlington local, with a double-deck coach at the rear, approaches Chicago in the summer of 1952. *J. M. Jarvis*

Left: The coffee-shop lounge car of the 'Empire Builder's' unique 'Ranch Car', and the lower-deck lounge of one of the train's dome cars, in the 1950s. *Great Northern Railway*

Above: Pre-Amtrak, Burlington Northern's 'North Coast Limited' at Livingston in July 1970. *V. Goldberg*

Right: An EMD road-switcher in Great Northern livery at Butte, Montana, in July 1970. *V. Goldberg*

electrification was in turn discontinued in 1956 when diesel traction took over. Another major new tunnel and lengthy re-alignment of the Great Northern route (by then, in fact, Burlington Northern) took place in 1970 with the construction of the Libby dam, in Western Montana.

On the West Coast, the GN had its main line from Seattle through Everett to the Canadian border at Blaine, and thence into Canada, partly over tracks shared with Canadian National, to its own station in Vancouver. The GN station was demolished in the late 1960s, after GN trains had been transferred to the CNR station. After a year (1971-72) during which the line was without passenger trains, international service was reintroduced under Amtrak sponsorship in July 1972.

At its easterly end, the GN reached Chicago over tracks of the Chicago, Burlington & Quincy Railroad (as did the Northern Pacific). Between St Paul and Minot, North Dakota (almost 500 miles),

the GN possessed two separate routes, and its branch-line coverage in northern North Dakota was particularly extensive, with over a dozen separate lines to the north, but all of them stopping short of the Canadian border. Their appearance on a map has given rise to the term 'picket fence country'. As with the Northern Pacific, the Great Northern had links from the twin lakehead ports to the Twin Cities and to Crookston. Minnesota, on the Winnipeg line, and to Grand Forks on the transcontinental route.

Jim Hill's construction of the Great Northern without Federal land grants (in contrast to the North Pacific), and his vigour in encouraging the settlement of immigrants in the country through which the GN passed, earned him the title of Empire Builder — the name also given to the principal transcontinental GN train in 1929, when it was refurbished. The *Empire Builder* was successor to the *Oriental Limited*, dating from 1905, which had a maritime extension in the form of

the GN steamship *Minnesota* (20,000 tons) linking Seattle with Japan and China. A further marine venture was the Great Northern Pacific Steamship Co (jointly owned by the GN and NP), which in 1915 inaugurated a service between Portland and San Francisco. The voyage took thirty hours, three hours less than the competing Southern Pacific's train !

The *Empire Builder* train became a streamliner in 1947, when five new train-sets (four owned by GN, and one by Chicago, Burlington & Quincy), ordered in 1943 but delayed by the war, entered service. The schedule of the new trains was forty-five hours between Chicago and the Pacific Northwest, thirteen and a half hours less than former timings. A further five new fifteen-car trains entered service in 1951, at which time the 1947 equipment and one further new train made up another revised and slightly slower schedule by the *Western Star.* In 1955, twenty-two dome-cars (six of them full-length Great Dome lounge cars) were added to the fleet. Both trains continued until the creation of Amtrak, which maintained operation of the *Empire Builder*, but via Milwaukee in the east and rerouted over the former North Pacific line to Seattle, west of Spokane.

The first *Empire Builder* streamlined trains introduced a colourful livery of bands of orange and green, separated by gold striping. In the 1960s the Great Northern introduced its Big Sky Blue livery, but it had by no means been fully applied by the time of the Burlington Northern merger, when a green livery was adopted.

Other GN passenger services operated until the formation of Amtrak included the picturesquely named *Badger* and *Gopher* trains linking the Twin Cities with *Duluth-Superior,* and a *Grand Forks-Winnipeg* train making connections with the *Western Star* at Grand Forks.

Although prominence is given here to the passenger services of both Great Northern and North Pacific, because

population along both lines has been relatively sparse, the roads have been predominantly freight carriers, with freight revenue outstripping that from passengers. Timber, agriculture and mines are the main sources of freight traffic, and NP was also a major landowner.

The Chicago, Burlington & Quincy Railroad, or Burlington Lines as it was known with its subsidiaries, was different. Although its mileage was greater than either of its parents — GN and NP acquired joint control in 1908 — it did not reach the Pacific. It did, however, form a link in the transcontinental route followed by the famed *California Zephyr* train, which, west of Denver, used the Denver & Rio Grande Western's short line to Salt Lake City. West from the Mormon capital, the tracks of the more recent Western Pacific, completed only in 1909, were used to reach the Pacific Ocean, or rather, the San Francisco Bay area at Oakland.

The CB&Q had its beginnings in the Aurora Branch Railroad, a spur off the short Galena & Chicago Union, which

became the foundation of the CB&Q's rival, the Chicago & North Western Railway. The Aurora built westward first to the Mississippi River (it adopted the title Chicago, Burlington & Quincy Railroad in 1855), forming a link with the Missouri river at St Joseph, via a ferry at Quincy, Illinois, and thence the Hannibal & St Joseph Railroad. A more northerly crossing of the Missouri was later made at Council Bluffs, Iowa (reached in 1870), whence the main line stretched west to Denver, 1,034 miles from Chicago. Other routes reached south to St Louis and to Kansas City; north from Aurora to the Twin Cities of Minneapolis-St Paul; and two lines to the north-west — one from Lincoln, Nebraska, the other from Denver, to reach Billings, Montana, on the Northern Pacific main line, where a Great Northern branch was also met.

On the Denver-Billings route, the 238 miles from Denver to Wendover, Wyoming, form the northern end of the Colorado & Southern Railway. Of the Southern's 718 miles, the 589 miles south

from Wendover to the Texas-New Mexico State line form part of a cross-country link from Denver to the Gulf of Mexico at Galveston, Texas. The 792 miles from Texline to Galveston are part of the 1,362-mile Fort Worth & Denver Railway, owned by the Colorado & Southern. The C & S in turn has been controlled by the Chicago, Burlington & Quincy since 1909. An interesting part, for a time, of the C & S system was the narrow-gauge (3ft) Denver, South Park & Pacific Railroad, built through rugged but scenic country, south-west from Denver, as a rival to the Denver & Rio Grande Western to tap Colorado's mines. Apart from one short spur, which was converted to standard gauge during the Second World War, the last leg of the Denver, South Pacific & Pacific Railroad, between Denver and Leadville, closed in 1937. The Colorado & Southern and Fort Worth & Denver are controlled by – but are not part of – Burlington Northern.

Although the Burlington (as the Chicago, Burlington & Quincy was often

called) was a leader in the western railroad passenger field, it, too, derived most of its income from freight. The Burlington's best-known contribution to the passenger market is probably the *Zephyr* title, afterwards carried by a whole fleet of high-speed trains. The pioneer *Zephyr* introduced in 1934 brought stainless-steel car-body construction, and successful diesel-electric traction, to the railroads. While the early articulated trains became an embarrassment because of their limited capacity, the basic designs were developed, and today's General Motors diesel locomotives and Budd stainless-steel locomotives and Budd stainless-steel passenger cars are the consequences of those early efforts.

Zephyrs raced in all directions, from Chicago to the Twin Cities, from Denver, to Dallas (*Texas Zephyr*) and on many other routes. The *Denver Zephyr*, with two full-length train-sets built in 1936, was one of the most successful. In 1956 the two twelve-car trains were replaced by new stock, the last completely new

Left: The 'Empire Builder' under Amtrak: two EMD Type SPD40F diesels, and baggage car still in Burlington Northern livery, at Minneapolis. *Amtrak*

Above: Road-rail container transfer terminal on Burlington Northern. *Burlington Northern Inc*

Below: 'Spokane River', seen at Fargo in July 1970, was one of the Great Northern 'Empire Builder's' sleepers. *V. Goldberg*

Bottom: Electric traction on the 'Cascadian' prepares to yield to steam at the end of the former Great Northern catenary at Skyomish for the run to Seattle in the 1940s. *Cecil J. Allen Collection*

train-sets to be built for US service until the advent of the Metroliners and experimental Turbotrains. Today, the route of the *Denver Zephyr* is still served by Amtrak's *San Francisco Zephyr* which proceeds from Denver over the Union Pacific to Ogden, and then over the Southern Pacific to Oakland.

The original trackage of the Chicago, Burlington & Quincy between Chicago and Aurora is, in addition, served by double-deck Gallery cars in commuter service, over a three-track section of the line. In 1972 the entire Burlington-Northern commuter equipment in the Chicago area was sold to the West Suburban Mass Transit District, which renewed and refurbished the carriage fleet, then leased it back to BN to continue operation.

The Spokane, Portland & Seattle Railway provides a 380-mile short cut, via the north bank of the Columbia River, for the Great Northern and North Pacific, from Spokane, Washington, to Portland, Oregon. The latter-day twice-daily (in each direction) passenger train service provided connections with transcontinental trains of both the NP and the GN. The SP & S owns two subsidiaries, the Oregon Trunk Railway from Wishram, Washington, to Bend, Oregon, and the Oregon Electric Railway (no longer electrified) from Portland to Eugene, Oregon. One small line, the Pacific Coast Railroad serving industries in the Seattle area, rounds off the Burlington Northern system.

Above: The 'California Zephyr' meets westbound freight on Burlington tracks at Naperville. *Blackhawk Films*

Right: Old wooden caboose newly decked in Burlington Northern livery in April 1971. *C. V. Ehrke*

Below: Amtrak's 'Empire Builder', before the days of SPD40F diesels, amid the superb scenery of Glacier National Park. *Amtrak*

CANADIAN PACIFIC & CANADIAN NATIONAL

A CANADIAN transcontinental railway was first proposed by an Imperial Commission in 1857, and a band of explorers spent four years in trying to map out a route. Although they discovered the Kicking Horse Pass (so named because a pack horse kicked a member of the party), through which the Canadian Pacific Railway was eventually to run, the difficulty posed by the great ranges of the Rockies and the Selkirks caused the leader of the party to report that 'the knowledge of the country as a whole would never lead me to advocate a line of communication from Canada across the continent to the Pacific'. In 1865 another survey party, organized by the Surveyor-General of British Columbia, carried out a more detailed exploration, and claimed to have discovered a practicable route.

Six more years passed before any further steps were taken. Until that time, Canada had been a loose association of provinces or colonies, generally acknowledging British rule, but one of them at least – British Columbia – was becoming extremely uneasy over its lack of communication with the rest of Canada. Indeed, British Columbia might have seceded to the United States had not the building of a transcontinental railway come urgently under review. The task to be faced was immense – first there were the rocky outcrops, muskegs and swamps in the almost uninhabited country west of Ottawa before Lake Superior could be reached. Then some difficult construction had to be undertaken round the cliffs bordering the lake. After that, hundreds of miles ran across prairie country to the great chain of the Rockies west of Calgary in Alberta. Finally there came 500 miles of fearsome mountain country through which track had to be laid.

The Canadian Pacific Railway was incorporated in February 1881 and before the end of the century included in its structure many railways in the provinces of Ontario and Quebec which had been in existence from the 1850s onwards. The new CPR, with the support of the Canadian government, began pushing eastwards and westwards from Winnipeg with such vigour that in no more than four years – five years before the obligatory date of completion of the railway – rail communication was established between Montreal, on the St Lawrence River, and Vancouver, British Columbia.

With the financial assistance of a number of distinguished men, and the driving power of William Van Horne, the laying of the line proceeded apace in both directions, and on 5 November 1885 the two tracks met at Craigellachie, in the heart of the Gold Range, where the last spike was driven. Such was the necessity

Below: Canadian National's 'Super Continental' in the Jasper area. *Canadian National Railways*

for completing the railway before funds ran out that in eighteen months from May 1882, no less than 675 miles of track were laid across the prairies to the junction of the Bow and Elbow rivers — the future site of Calgary — with a maximum of 6 miles 660 yards in a single day.

On 23 May 1887 the first Canadian Pacific Railway train from the east ran into Vancouver. The one-and-a-half-year interval since completion had been occupied in improving the hastily laid track so that trains could make the through journey safely. Because it had been essential to get the service going at the earliest possible moment, a good deal of the original construction, especially through the three ranges of the Rocky Mountains, was of a temporary nature. The intention was to replace the provisional structures by others of a permanent character as soon as the railway was earning money and adequate time could be given to the reconstructions. Over many mountain ravines the railway was carried on great timber-trestle viaducts, built from wood cut in the adjacent forests. The greatest of the trestle viaducts, across Stoney Creek, was later replaced by a massive steel arch.

Some of the improvements were more costly. After the line had dropped from the Kicking Horse Pass down to the gorge of the Columbia River at Golden, the river's great bend to the northwards meant too great a diversion, so a route was taken through the Selkirk Mountains to reach the river again at Revelstoke. It involved a tortuous climb on one in forty-five gradients to the 4,350 feet altitude of the Rogers Pass, four and a half miles of which had to be protected by timber snowsheds in order to avoid blocking the line in winter. Later, a bold decision was made to cut out the difficult section by tunnelling under Mount Macdonald. This five-mile bore lowered the railway's summit by 540 feet and, for a cost of £1,125,000, vastly improved the operating over the section when the Connaught Tunnel was opened in 1916.

Another costly improvement affected the descent westwards down the Yoho Valley from the 5,329 feet altitude of the Great Divide. To hasten construction, the original line was carried straight down the valley on a ruling gradient of one in twenty-three. That proved a serious handicap to trains having to climb in the eastbound direction, while in the westbound direction care was needed to prevent trains from running away down so steep an incline. An entirely new route was, therefore, adopted, which reduced the gradient from one in twenty-three to one in forty-five, and was brought into use in 1909. On the new route trains starting the descent enter a spiral tunnel from which they emerge at a level lower by fifty-four feet, and travel-

Top: CP Pacific No 2470 leaves Montreal's Windsor Street station in 1959. *J. N. Westwood*

Left: CN 2-8-2 No 3709 heads freight at Portland, Maine. *J. M. Jarvis*

ling in the opposite direction. After crossing the river and the former route, which is now a road, they enter a similar tunnel in the opposite mountainside to emerge at a still lower level and heading in the original direction. The relocation has added several miles to the distance covered, of course, but halving the steepness of the descent has made a great difference to the operation. The route closely resembles that at Wassen on the Gotthard Railway of Switzerland.

Canadian National, unlike Canadian Pacific, was not conceived as a nationwide system, although some of its principal components eventually grew to meet that description. The formation of CNR took place in stages in the period 1918-23. The new system included three major elements (and several minor constituents), namely, the Canadian Northern Railway (CNoR), a Canadian enterprise; the Canadian Government Railways (CGR), in public ownership; and the Grand Trunk Railway (GTR), an English-owned system.

The Grand Trunk was the oldest established of the three, and included Canada's first railway, the Champlain & St Lawrence, a portage railway linking the St

Above right: A CP business car of traditional North American outline alongside the transcontinental 'Canadian' at Thunder Bay, Fort William, Ontario, in July, 1970. *V. Goldberg*

Right: CP's eastbound 'Dominion' leaves Rogers Pass in the Selkirk Mountains, summit of the transcontinental line, in February, 1963. *J. G. Tawse*

Below: An oncoming 4-4-4 of the semi-streamlined jubilee class, built for Canadian Pacific in 1936-38. *Blackhawk Films*

Overleaf: CP's 'Canadian' near the Great Divide in the Rockies, with Mount Cathedral dominating the scene. *CP Rail*

Lawrence River, opposite Montreal, with the Lake Champlain river system at St Johns. Built to a gauge of 5ft 6in, it opened on 21 July 1836, with an English locomotive, *Dorchester,* four American coaches and Montreal-built wagons. For several decades, the 5ft 6in gauge was widely used in Canada, and it was adopted by the Grand Trunk Railway when it opened in 1856. The GTR was intended to be a main line linking Upper and Lower Canada (Ontario and Quebec), and was built to high standards. Extensions to its main line between Toronto and Montreal, and the take-over of other companies, eventually brought it west to Chicago in the USA, and east to Quebec and beyond. All its track was converted to standard gauge by 1874. However, the railway was not an unqualified success financially, despite its 4,800 route-miles.

Two late-Victorian Canadian entrepreneurs, William MacKenzie and Donald Mann, founded the Canadian Northern Railway. From a small group of lines in Manitoba, the CNoR expanded, in less than two decades, to an 8,000-mile transcontinental system, mostly of new construction, but incorporating some existing local lines. Growth was encouraged by swelling immigration, but it was supported also by the wish of the public and government that transcontinental traffic should not be wholly

some of its components had earlier been built to the 5ft 6in gauge. Its route lay close to the shore of the St Lawrence, well away from the United States border. The ICR was a sizeable unit of the Canadian Government Railways, but the National Transcontinental Railway (NTR) was longer. Its route – deliberately circuitous to open up formerly untapped areas – ran through Northern Ontario and Quebec, linking Winnipeg with Quebec City, and on east to Moncton, New Brunswick.

A subsidiary of the Grand Trunk, the Grand Trunk Pacific (GTP) was built west from Winnipeg, to reach the Pacific at the new port of Prince Rupert, through much country ready for immediate development. The completion in 1915 of this new transcontinental route (which was built from the start to main-line standards) followed the outbreak of the First World War. In consequence, the tide of immigrants upon which the newly opened railways depended ceased, with dire consequences for much of Canada's railway network. The wartime traffic boom came only in already developed areas; Halifax, Nova Scotia, for example, became a vital port in the route to Europe.

The new lines, the Canadian Northern, the National Transcontinental and the Grand Trunk Pacific, quickly experienced financial problems – such that the CNoR

of Prince Edward Island were sponsored by the island's government, and a 3ft 6in-gauge system developed there from 1874 had reached a mileage of 278 by 1912. In an island only 120 miles long, and never more than twenty-five miles wide, such intensive coverage caused financial problems from the start, and a condition of the entry of Prince Edward Island to the dominion in 1873 was that the dominion assumed responsibility for the PEI Railway. It was placed in the hands of the Intercolonial Railway and eventually became part of the Canadian National Railway. Conversion to standard gauge was spread over the period 1919-30. Today, train ferries link the island with the mainland, and although passenger services have recently ceased, the aura of the narrow gauge lingers on in the island.

Newfoundland is an island the size of England. It claims to be Britain's oldest colony and Canada's newest province. The railway came late to 'Newfie' – 1884 – but eventually over 900 miles of 3 ft 6in-gauge track crossed the island, and branched out to some of the costal communities. Of narrow gauge to this day, the system, after a chequered career, first in private hands and then under the Newfoundland Government, passed to CNR when Newfoundland joined the confederation in 1949. Although the

dependent on the Canadian Pacific.

Canada is unique in its railways in possessing, side by side, two major systems; one publicly owned, the other in private hands. Early examples of public ownership (and, indeed, construction) were found in the maritime colonies of Nova Scotia and New Brunswick. A rail link with Canada East and West (i.e. Lower and Upper Canada) was a requirement for the inclusion of those colonies in the Dominion of Canada, just as British Columbia needed the construction of the Canadian Pacific.

The Intercolonial Railway, (ICR) as the eastern link became, was completed in 1875 as a standard-gauge line, although

passed to the control of the Canadian Government Railway late in 1918. The combined system came to be known as Canadian National Railways early in 1919, and the Grand Trunk Pacific, after being placed in receivership in that year, came under CNR management in 1920. Management of the Grand Trunk Railway itself passed in 1922 to the CNR and late the same year the name Canadian National Railways was formally adopted. In January 1923, all the constituents were legally amalgamated.

Most of the CNR components had included smaller secondary railways taken over in a variety of circumstances. Among them, railways in the then colony

line's mileage has shrunk to 700 and passenger service is confined now to mixed trains, CN's nearest approach to Britain is an area of great interest. Train ferries provide a link with the island's increasing freight traffic, and freight can be transhipped at Port aux Basques, the island ferry terminal, or trucks (bogies) can be changed on dual-gauge sidings.

The major traffic centres and focal points of Canadian National Railway are Moncton (for the Maritime provinces),

Far left: CN 4-8-4 No 6402 pulls out of Toronto in April 1952. *J. M. Jarvis*

Above right: The diner 'Arcadian', typifying the 1954-55 Budd-built equipment of CP's 'Canadian' at Thunder Bay. *V. Goldberg*

Right: The westbound 'Canadian' makes a late evening call at Chalk River, Ontario, in July 1970. *V. Goldberg*

Below: Toronto (left) and Montreal sections of CN's eastbound 'Panorama' transcontinental ready to go their separate ways from Capreol, Ontario. *J. G. Tawse*

Montreal and Toronto (for Quebec and Ontario respectively) and Winnipeg, for the Prairie provinces. The principal freight marshalling yards are located at these four points — with many other yards elsewhere.

In the passenger field, CN had one of the better timetables in North America for many years. With a system route-mileage of 23,500, and many hundreds of miles of new lines built since the war, this is, perhaps, not surprising. In addition to transcontinental service linking Montreal and Toronto with Vancouver, CN serves the 'trunk' corridor Quebec-Montreal-Toronto-SW Ontario, where the larger parts of Canada's population, industry and agriculture are located.

The system's headquarters are in Montreal, where the modern Central station provides appropriate facilities for the traveller. There, also, is the only electrified part of the system, an eighteen-mile suburban line, with a three-mile-long tunnel under Mount Royal, equipped with a 2,400V dc overhead system.

Toronto has some suburban rail service along the lake-shore, provided by CN over its tracks under contract to the Government of Ontario, with the title GO Transit. On its own account, CN operates a few local trains around Toronto. Other areas of passenger activity include the Maritimes, served by the well-known *Ocean Limited* and the *Scotian* trains, and northern areas were there are few highways.

Rolling stock on Canadian National Railways has followed North American practice for many years, although a number of English features were in evidence in early days. With so many different constituents, the steam locomotive fleet was quite varied. At its peak it numbered 3,260 locomotives, but the figure later settled down to about 2,500. Perhaps best known were upwards of two hundred 4-8-4s, half of which dated from the 1940s, and most of which survivied to the end of steam in 1960. In order of totals, 2-8-0s (850), 2-8-2s (500), 4-6-0s (600) and Pacifics (330) made up most of the fleet, with other types less in evidence. A particularly Canadian feature in more recent construction was the fully enclosed cab to provide protection against the northern winter. Dieselization took place late (compared with the USA) and quickly, in the period 1951-60.

Passenger stock also followed conventional North American practice. A change from all-over dark green to an attractive green-gold-black livery coincided in 1953 with a huge $59,000,000 order for over 350 modern streamlined passenger coaches in the mid-1950s, one of the biggest ever placed by a North American railroad. A few years later, a modern corporate style was adopted, with a new CN device and passenger coaches finished in black and white, with bright reds and blues internally.

This visual transformation was the first step taken by a CN administration determined to bring the public's view of the railroad up to date by modern methods of marketing and revitalized service. Early in the 1960s CN followed up with an all-out bid to entice passengers out of automobiles and planes back into trains. Journeys were accelerated. The Montreal-Toronto *Rapidos*, in particular, were cut to a 4 hours 59 minutes schedule for the 335 miles, which made them the fastest regular services in North America; and the Montreal-Vancouver *Super Continental*, introduced in 1955, came down to its best-ever westbound timing of 68 hours 40 minutes. For four years from 1967 to 1971, CN was bold enough to run two transcontinentals daily, the other being the *Panorama*. To promote this vigorous new service, CN launched a 'Red, White and Blue' ticket structure which substantially discounted fares in off-peak periods.

At first CN's adventurous approach seemed to be wholly justified. Within a year most routes were reporting passenger-mileage increases ranging from forty per cent to more than sixty per cent, and revenue was up encouragingly, too — though nowhere near enough to erase CN's overall passenger service deficit. Soon, CN had insufficient modern cars to cope with the extra business, so it turned to the USA for redundant streamliner equipment, such as ex-*Hiawatha Skytop* observation-sleeper cars and domes for the Montreal-Halifax *Ocean Limited*. At the same time it arranged a lease with United Aircraft for five seven-car Turbotrains to reduce the Montreal-Toronto transit time to 4 hours 10 minutes — a deal which was initially disastrous. And in 1967 it bought attractive new lightweight train-sets for the *Tempo* service between Toronto, Sarnia and Windsor.

All this was the more striking because by then Canadian Pacific had written off the inter-city passenger train as a dying, if not altogether dead, service. A mark of the CP attitude was the 1965 agreement to end the 1933 arrangement whereby, originally to cut costs during the Depression, CP and CN had pooled equipment and receipts on the key Montreal-Toronto and Montreal-Quebec routes. Henceforward CP was happy to relinquish the Montreal-Toronto and Toronto-Ottawa routes exclusively to CN.

But all CN's efforts could not close the gap between passenger costs and receipts. Their sparkling show of speed and style on a few prime routes did not mask the equipment's age elsewhere and the general lack of train speed compared with road and air competition. After all, the *Super Continental* averaged no better than 42mph throughout its 2,914-mile run from Montreal to Vancouver, and was limited by the state of the track to 75mph. The multi-coloured fare scheme may have filled some seats that would otherwise have been empty, but it was not generating enough extra revenue to keep pace with the mounting costs of further improvements to the service.

By the close of the 1960s CN and CP

Facing page: A CP unit train moves sulphur from Alberta through the Rockies near Banff en route for Vancouver and export shipment. *CP Rail*

Below: A Government of Ontario Transit train working GO-sponsored suburban service in the Toronto area at Oakville in May 1968. *J. K. Hayward*

Centre: Budd RDC diesel railcar in CP service between Toronto and Windsor in May 1971, at West Toronto. *V. Goldberg*

Bottom: A photograph taken at a well-known spiral tunnel in 1968 displays the freight vehicle liveries that CP had just introduced as part of its new corporate identity. *CP Rail*

were seeking to curtail their passenger services. As the 1970s wore on, both public and Government grew anxious at the rising costs of subsidizing the country's rail passenger services — by 1975 the support was climbing towards $150,000,000 annually — and there was talk of semi-nationalization, Amtrak-style. One economy particularly canvassed was an end to the daily competitive service of the two lavishly-equipped and staffed transcontinental trains, CN's *Super Continental* and CP's *Canadian.*

At last, in the spring of 1977, the Canadian Government put rail passenger services on a new footing. Although neither CN nor CP would be relieved of their statutory duty to run passenger trains, the services would be segregated from the rest of the railroad operations; amalgamated and rationalized under the management of new company, Via Canada Rail Inc (VIA for short); and separately accounted and budgeted under Government supervision. Although VIA is a subsidiary of CN, its board includes CP men, and representatives of the Government, of commerce and of trade unions.

VIA was actually a creature of CN — in fact, it was part of the armour in CN's strenuous campaign of 1976 to persuade the Canadian Government to relieve the railroads of their $50,000,000-a-year passenger losses. VIA's symbol was quickly applied to a whole host of CN passenger items, ranging from conduc-

tors' buttons and timetables to snack-bar napkins. On the Turbotrains it was complemented by a vivid new gold and blue livery, a variation of which was to adorn other CN passenger equipment too. Until 1977, though, VIA was purely a CN exercise.

So Canadian passenger trains are to be visually restyled yet again in a fresh attempt to persuade the Canadian public to travel by rail. A two-year moratorium on service closures is possible while VIA finds its operational feet, and also while the Government decides which services to cut as insupportably expensive, or as adequately covered by alternative transport; which parallel CN and CP services to rationalize; and which services to develop. However, the Government now openly shoulders the responsibility for the character and financing of former CN and CP rail passenger services. The Ministry of Transport will gradually select the routes to be retained, then will enter into fixed-term contracts with VIA to operate them. VIA, in turn, will plan the timetables, contract with CN and CP for the necessary traction and train crews, and market the resultant train services. The Government has emphasized that it would pay sufficient cash on its contracts with VIA to give the new company every incentive to create an attractive product.

At the time of writing, two fresh developments in Canadian rail passenger service are certain to follow. One is that,

probably by mid-1978, the transcontinentals will be partly merged. Separate trains will still originate in Montreal and Toronto and run individually to Sudbury, but there they will combine for the run to Winnipeg as one train. At Winnipeg they will be split again, to give passengers a choice of CP or CN scenic routes on to Vancouver. The other assured event is a high-speed demonstration project in the Montreal-Quebec corridor.

The Canadian Government put up $30,000,000 to launch the Montreal-Quebec exercise in the spring of 1976, with a promise of $90,000,000 to extend the project throughout the Quebec-Windsor corridor if the pilot enterprise proved economically successful. Work on the track and signalling was to be finished by the end of 1979. Train-sets, which will be owned by the Canadian Government, are to be the 125 mph LRC, developed by a consortium of Canadian industries under the leadership of Alcan Canada with financial support from the Government (the LRC is described in the earlier chapter of this book, 'Railcars and Lightweight Trains').

Neither CN nor CP is exclusively a railroad operator. CN has a hotel chain in principal cities, and its coastal shipping activities are extensive, particularly in the

east. Newfoundland's coast is well served, and several ferry services are operated elsewhere on the Atlantic seaboard. The SS *Prince George* provides a link with Alaska on the Pacific, and a barge service to link up with CN's isolated freight lines on Vancouver Island. CN is also active in the field of telecommunications, and until recently, 'fathered' the national airline Air Canada.

CP is even more diversified. The activities of this big conglomerate includes international air and shipping services, vast mining and property interests and telecommunications, road haulage and hotel services, in addition to its railways. Even so, CP railways today still cover some 16,500 miles of route.

An outstanding CP freight operation is its bulk movement of export coal from Kaiser Coal's mines at Crowsnest Pass, on the western slopes of the Rocky Mountains, to Roberts Bank, a port on the Straits of Georgia about twenty miles south of Vancouver. Six trains of eighty-eight hoppers, each with up to 11,000-12,000 tons gross capacity when fully loaded, are in continuous circuit on the extremely arduous 693-mile route from the British Columbia mines to the port and back.

Each loaded run is a six-stage operation. At the mine the rail layout is a loop

bridged by overhead bunkers, so that an arriving empty train needs no reversal but, headed by four 3,000hp diesel locomotives with special 'creep control', is loaded as it crawls non-stop under the bunkers at an unvarying half mile an hour. The 'creep control' diesels continue to haul the train for some 220 miles down the slopes to the CP transcontinental main line at Golden. Here they are replaced by orthodox diesels at the front, while at suitable intervals in the train two pairs of 'slave' diesels are inserted. The 'slaves' are unmanned locomotives remotely controlled from the manned cabs at the head end by radio links which keep their power and brake controls precisely in step with those of the leading locomotives. At Beavermouth, twenty-eight miles further west, the line begins a fierce climb over the Selkirk Mountains, for which three locomotives are attached as bankers, so that the train now has some 33,000hp pulling and pushing. At Stoney Creek, just before the five-mile Connaught Tunnel under Mount Macdonald, the bankers are detached; and en route to Roberts Bank two more stops are made to reduce the head-end and 'slave' power as the inclines ease. Each of the six trains in the circuit is programmed to complete an out-and-home trip every seventy-two hours.

So important is this traffic, and such is the volume of freight generally which rail moves over the Rockies, that in 1977 CP decided, despite the cost, to double the track at several places between Calgary and Vancouver. In the wild Beaver River Valley stretch east of Rogers Pass this may even necessitate boring a new eight-mile tunnel beneath the existing five-mile Connaught Tunnel. The aim of this project is to increase capacity, and to create a more easily graded path for loaded westbound trains.

In equipment, CP was unusual in North America in building its own steam locomotives and passenger coaches. Its Delorimier and, later, Angus shops, both in Montreal, built quality products of traditional designs. Of the steam locomotive fleet (which numbered 1,962 in 1937) the large Selkirks (2-10-4s) and Royal Hudsons (4-6-4s) were best known, but numerous workaday 2-8-2s and 2-8-0s provided the backbone for freight service. For secondary lines, a large fleet of 4-6-0s powered trains across the system. Much of the passenger equipment was of conventional heavyweight construction, but advanced smooth-sided coaches were introduced in the 1930s.

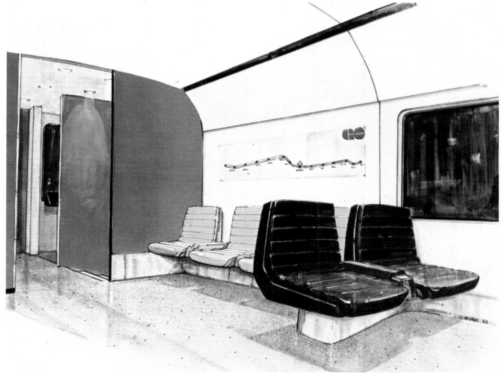

Left: CN's 'Super Continental' at Jasper, Alberta, with Mount Fitzwilliam in the background. *Canadian National Railways*

Above right: Bombardier-MLW's new-look prototype LRC diesel-electric power car and trailer hit 129mph during a fast run east of Montreal on 10 March 1976.

Right: Artist's impression of the interior of passenger stock specially built for the GO Transit service in the Toronto area.

Below: An ex-Milwaukee 'Skyview' observation lounge, which used to bring up the rear of the 'Olympian Hiawatha' and went into CN's 'Ocean' and 'Scotian' between Montreal and Halifax. *Canadian National Railways*

HAS AMTRAK REBORN THE PASSENGER TRAIN?

THE NORTH AMERICAN inter-city passenger train seemed doomed to oblivion in the 1960s. Battered by competition from airline, automobile and bus, the passenger train network had shrunk to five hundred or so trains daily by the end of the 1960s, compared with its peak of around 15,000 in 1936-41.

Many people argued that it wasn't the absent riders who were killing the passenger train. The railroads, they maintained, were the culprits with their curtailment of amenities, penny-pinching lack of investment and defective — or totally deficient — marketing. Practically every railroad complained it was losing vast sums of money on passenger service and produced statistics to prove it. But critics asserted that passenger trains were loaded with far more than their fair share of joint costs — general expenses of track,

staff, signalling and so on, which no one has yet been able to allocate accurately between one sort of train and another. They accused the majority of railroads of wanting to suppress passenger trains simply to concentrate on easier and more lucrative freight movement.

Could the USA learn to live without the passenger train? Anxiously aware of its overcrowded airlanes and fume-choked cities and highways, a growing body of public opinion thought not — and said so loudly, for everyone was turning an ear to the ecologists. In that case, countered the railroads, someone else must meet the bill.

Throughout 1969 an assortment of schemes to rescue and support inter-city passenger service financially was considered by both Houses of Congress. Towards the end of the year the Nixon

administration promised to table its own plan, but by March 1970 it had not done so. Already it was clear that the Department of Transportation and the White House Office of Management and Budget were at loggerheads over the concept of Government-financed take-over of passenger train operation. Irritated at the administration's delays, the Senate Commerce Committee put through its own Bill to establish a National Railroad Passenger Corporation, which it proposed to launch with a $435,000,000 subsidy. That offensive word subsidy at last stung the Republican administration to seek a compromise.

Even so, when the final Bill passed both Houses of Congress in October 1970, staff at the White House urged a Presidential veto, which the Transportation Department and the railroads had to

struggle to resist. To the end, the Office of Management and Budget fought to restrict the number of routes to be operated by the corporation, insisting that none must be nominated without OMB approval. For different reasons, the railroad unions too were trying to block or delay the new regime. But at last, at midnight on 30 April 1971, the old order yielded. 'Railpax' (for National Railroad Passenger Corporation), as the new organization had been called, became Amtrak (for *Am*erica, *Tr*avel and Tr*ack*) just before the take-over.

Some 300 passenger trains ceased to exist that night, for any railroad joining Amtrak was entitled to discontinue all its inter-city – but not commuter – passenger services immediately, except those Amtrak chose to maintain and pay for. As Amtrak's first timetable listed only 184 trains on twenty-one routes, some 300 had been eliminated at a stroke. Any railroad rejecting the Amtrak deal (outstanding were Southern, Denver & Rio Grande Western, and Rock Island) was required to keep its existing services going, at the current standards of service, for two years at least.

A railroad's entrance fee to Amtrak was either half the total of its losses on passenger service in 1969; or a sum equivalent to its otherwise avoidable losses in running passenger trains in 1969; or twice the latter amount in respect of such of its services as Amtrak was to take over. The fee could be paid in either cash or equipment, such as locomotives and cars

to create Amtrak trains. For its part, Amtrak was to pay its railroad hosts appropriately for operating its trains and terminals, plus a five per cent margin, and issue common stock to them in return for their entry payments. Those down payments totalled around $200,000,000, to which Government direct grants and

Government-guaranteed loans added $40,000,000 and $100,000,000 respectively – not an excessively large sum on which to found a revitalized national inter-city passenger system, especially as Amtrak was committed to work for a profit. Moreover, though Amtrak was freed from the restriction of having to seek approval from the Interstate Commerce Commission for every passenger service modification, it could not escape another burden: its founding Act required it to respect all existing labour agreements.

Certain standards were set for Amtrak services by Nixon's Transportation Secretary, John Volpe. There had to be through car service between the ends of each nominated route and services should connect at terminals (the time required before a connection degenerated into a stopover was not precisely defined). Trains had to run at times of popular demand and as fast as track and equipment allowed – which, as time went on, was to be a crucially limiting qualification. Further provisions pronounced that trains on the move six hours and more between midnight and 08.00 must have

private-room sleeping-cars; trains moving at least two hours between 07.00 and 20.00 must serve food; and trains on the move for six hours or more must include supplementary lounge accommodation.

At the start, things were much as they had been, except that the trains were

Left: A Turboliner built in France and imported by Amtrak. *Amtrak*

Above: Two of Amtrak's ill-starred SPD40F diesels head the 'Coast Starlight' near San Luis Obispo in California. *Amtrak*

fewer and shorter (largely because Amtrak had not taken over the mail business previously carried by passenger trains). For its opening, Amtrak had no new equipment. For traction, it could only lease the ageing E- and F-cab diesels made redundant by the railroads' abandonment of their own passenger services, and buy up some 1,200 of their newest passenger cars. Many trains were a bright collection of several former owners' liveries, but otherwise looked much the same as before, until in 1972 Amtrak started to refurbish and repaint its fleet in its own red, white and blue style with its arrow-type symbol. To be fair to the first Amtrak managers, one must remember that in the early days they were not wholly sure whether the administration expected Amtrak to preside over a gentle, face-saving extinction of the passenger train or to mount an exciting resurrection.

By the spring of 1972 Amtrak felt sufficiently assured to become more venturesome. The timetable had been built up to a daily 215 trains; rail passenger service was being actively marketed ('We're making the trains fun to ride again', ran the best-known advertisement); smartly costumed hostesses were persuasive evidence that someone was caring again, and the passengers were returning, albeit slowly. Some historic trains were improved and others revived, like the former Illinois Central *Panama Limited* from Chicago to New Orleans. There was sensible rationalization, such as the concentration of Chicago's long-haul trains on just one depot, the Union. And there were bids to broach new markets, as with the winter gambling specials run from Los Angeles to Las Vegas and ski-ing specials to Sun Valley, Idaho, both over Union Pacific routes.

Apart from its early handicap of antiquated equipment (and the initial disinterest of the two major car-builders in reopening their assembly lines) Amtrak had the problem of variable treatment from its host railroads. Some railroad men at all levels resented Amtrak, or at best grumbled at an expensive nuisance. Amtrak's well-publicized good intentions could so easily be thwarted by disinterested or surly train staff who made their own rules about meal service, or by operators who marshalled observation cars in the middle of a train instead of at the end, or accorded their own freight trains priority. One of Amtrak's biggest problems was that railroads were under no obligation to make trunk routes that were battered by heavy freight trains fit for fast passenger trains; as the railroads had to foot the bill, they naturally did as little as possible.

To Amtrak's amazed delight, the Senate Appropriations Committee doubled the funds the corporation modestly sought in 1972. That allowed Amtrak to cut short its modernization of leased E-cab diesels to fifty out of 113 units, write the Fs out of its forward plans and buy new equipment.

The first fruits in traction were 150 3,000hp Electromotive SPD40F diesel-electrics, a cowled-cab unit with full-width body based on the FP45 produced by Electromotive to a Santa Fe specification in 1967. Ordered in batches, the SPD40Fs were delivered to Amtrak in lots in 1973-74 and became Amtrak's standard long-haul power. Six roads maintained them on Amtrak's behalf — Santa Fe, Burlington Northern, Illinois Central Gulf, Conrail (formerly Penn-Central), Seaboard Coast Line, and Southern Pacific. At first, Amtrak rejoiced in the SPD40Fs, but all too soon they were to be a significant factor in Amtrak's 1976-77 winter crisis.

The pride of Amtrak in its formative years was the high-speed Metroliner service on ex-Penn-Central tracks in the North-East Corridor between New York and Washington. It was so popular and profitable that Amtrak intensified the operation to fourteen trains each way daily. The modern Budd-built coaches of these self-contained electric train-sets had 125mph capability and were so adaptable to different internal configurations that Amtrak decided to make the car the basis of a new short- and medium-haul fleet. In all, 492 new cars were con-

Top: Close up of a General Electric Type E60CP electric locomotive. *Amtrak*

Centre: An EMD Type F40PH diesel heads Amfleet cars on the 'Senator' in Connecticut. *Amtrak*

Bottom: Near view of an EMD Type SPD40F diesel. *Amtrak*

structed. They were given the name Amfleet, and the different models were called Amcoach, Amcafé, Amdinette, Amlounge, and so on, to match. That disgusted many enthusiasts who affectionately remembered the euphonious names of individual cars in days gone by.

The SPD40F diesels had been arranged to power the steam-heating and air-conditioning of Amtrak's original car fleet. The new Amfleet cars, however, were all-electric and needed traction with head-end power to match. So Amtrak bought two more new diesel types: from General Electric, twenty-five P30CH 3,000hp units, derived from the U30CG and U36CH built by GE for Santa Fe and Erie-Lackawanna respectively; and from Electromotive, thirty 3,000hp F40PH units, a brand-new member of the SPD40F family – but, most importantly, mounted on four all-powered axles, not six like the SPD40F and P30CH. Turboliners apart, Amtrak's traction purchases were rounded off by procuring from General Electric twenty-six new E60CP locomotives to supersede the Pennsylvania GG1s on the electrified stretches of the Boston-New York-Washington corridor.

Finally, Amtrak secured 284 more new cars to take over from the pre-Amtrak stock on the long hauls, such as Chicago to the Pacific Coast and New Orleans to California. This time Amtrak worked out a brand-new design, though one that bore a resemblance to Santa Fe's Budd-built Hi-Level equipment, because of its double-deck configuration. But Amtrak's new bi-level Superliners, at 16ft 2in, are 7½in higher than the Santa Fe cars, carry more passengers on the two levels, yet are lighter because their all-electric auxiliaries, like air-conditioning, are fed

from a generator on the locomotive. Other features of the Superliners are ramps for handicapped passengers, tracked seats to allow easy adjustment, air-cushion suspension bogies of German design and 120mph capability.

The 249 Superliners ordered from Pullman-Standard include mixed-class sleepers (first-class de luxe bedrooms with private shower on the upper storey, economy rooms below), all-economy sleepers, standard reclining-seat day cars, diners – and a modern version of the dome: the Sightseer-Lounge, with a twenty-six-seater café/bar-lounge on the lower deck and on the upper a forty-six-seater bar lounge with electric piano, beneath a fully-glazed roof. However, because of the standard roof height of all Superliners there is no view fore and aft from the upper-floor lounge of a Sightseer as there is in the old-style dome – another irritation among the traditionalists.

With all this new traction and passenger equipment delivered, 'one-half of all inter-city train travellers in the USA were riding in the best, most advanced cars that technology can provide', boasted Amtrak President Paul H. Reistrup. That, he added, hadn't pertained even in the golden age of the inter-city streamliner after the Second World War – and Amtrak was far from finished yet.

Although expenditure was already close on $550,000,000, at the start of 1977 Reistrup handed newly-elected President Carter a five-year plan that would very nearly cost another $600,000,000: proposed purchases indicated 153 more Superliners for the Chicago-Texas *Inter-American* and *Lone Star*, the Chicago-New Orleans *Panama Limited* and Chicago-Florida *Floridian*;

118 second-generation Metroliners for the Boston-New York-Washington service; 365 new long-haul single-level cars for services where overhead electric wires and tunnels prohibit the Superliners, such as the New York-Chicago *Broadway Limited* and New York-Florida trains; 105 more 3,000hp diesels to supersede Amtrak's remaining vintage Es and Fs; 15 diesel switchers; and 30 new electrics to replace the remaining Pennsylvania GG1s in the North-East Corridor. These last might not be more of the GE Class E60Cs. Their introduction was startlingly deferred for ten months after one of them had been derailed in their early days at speed in 1975, after which they had to be gradually eased back by modification to their originally planned 100mph-plus maximum. The cash penalty which General Electric had to pay for failure to deliver on time in good order did not help to dispel the unpleasantness of that experience.

New electric locomotives were one product for which Amtrak were inclined to buy foreign expertise. In the spring of 1977 Amtrak men were delighted by two samples of European technology leased for trial. One was a four-axle 4,850hp Swedish State Railways Class Rc-4 locomotive, built by the Swedish firm ASEA, an electric rail-traction market-leader in Europe which has made a speciality of thyristor control systems. The attraction of the Swedish machine was that it weighed only half the tonnage of the 6,000hp GE E60CP (though

Below: An E60CP electric locomotive heads Amfleet cars in the North-East Corridor. *Amtrak*

Overleaf: A New York-Washington Metroliner in Amtrak colours. *Amtrak*

admittedly it did not arrive fitted with the motor-alternator set which the E60CP carries to power electrically the Amfleet cars' auxiliaries). Computerized data showed that the ASEA locomotive would come within a minute or two at most of the General Electric locomotive's predicted timing on a New York-Washington run with five intermediate stops, at a limit of 110mph after the route's renovation.

The other engine on trial in the North-East Corridor was French: one of the dual-frequency 25kV ac/1.5kV dc six-axle locomotives which French Railways employ on international expresses between Paris and the Franco-Swiss fron-

tier at Vallorbe. This locomotive, however, was sent back quite soon – primarily because its suspension could not adjust to the vagaries of poorly-maintained USA track, compared with the permanent way in its own country, and the technical difficulties of modifying it to suit American conditions.

Amtrak also leased for a two-year trial a pair of Canada's trains of the future, the LRC (for *L*ight, *R*apid, *C*omfortable, or *Léger, Rapide, Confortable*). Developed by a consortium of Canadian industries, the low-slung, diesel-alternator-powered LRC is a lightweight that makes substantial use of aluminium alloy stressed-skin techniques in the construction of its bodywork. Designed for 125mph operation, it is one of the numerous high-speed train designs which incorporates an automatic body-tilting mechanism so as to allow faster negotiation of curves without discomfort to passengers. Amtrak was delighted with its performance at 90mph on a curve where conventional equipment is limited to 60mph. One unit has already been worked up to a Canadian rail speed record of 124.5mph on Canadian Pacific's Adirondack subdivision, east of Montreal. The LRC was also given a lengthy evaluation at the Pueblo test centre before Amtrak's decision to take two for service trials. The Canadians intend the LRC to operate as a double-ended set with a 2,900hp power car (a product of MLW-Worthington) at each end, but Amtrak's two sets comprise just one power and five passenger cars apiece. Their likely assignment is the Vancouver-Seattle-Portland route and Amtrak has an option on ten more LRCs at the conclusion of the two-year trial period.

Left: The counter of an Amcafé car. *Amtrak*

Above: Amcoach accommodation in Amfleet equipment. *Amtrak*

Right: The US-built version of the French RTG gas turbine train-set constructed by Rohr. Comparison with the picture on page 106 shows the differences in detail. *Amtrak*

Overleaf: Artist's impressions of the accommodation planned for Amtrak's new double-deck Superliner cars for long hauls: upper level of sightseer lounge: diner; and family sleeper. *Amtrak*

Most striking of all Amtrak's acquisitions to date is a whole railway – the vital North-East Corridor from Boston via New York and Philadelphia to Washington, which carries fifty per cent of Amtrak's passengers. The inability of the impoverished Penn-Central to keep the track of this key route fit for 100mph Metroliners, let alone improve it for still higher speed, had been a difficulty from Amtrak's conception. When Conrail was formed, it was to be charged with the job in return for a realistic fee from Amtrak for use of the railroad. But the 4R Act of 1975 allowed Amtrak to buy the route complete – which it did, for the $87,000,000 that the USRA deemed fair liquidation value but which the Penn-Central trustees, creditors and shareholders protested was derisory. So Amtrak is now the North-East Corridor's manager and operator, and Conrail leases use of the tracks for its freight.

At the same time the Department of Transportation secured Congressional passage, and President Ford's endorsement, of a Bill approving modernization of the route at a cost of $1,600,000,000:

ninety per cent of the money would be Federal, the rest would come from the eight States adjoining the corridor. Amtrak was striving for a 160mph super-railway, but the Ford administration flatly refused to accept the staggering costs that would have incurred. Even the scaled-down estimates for a 125mph route were snubbed, for the Ford administration and especially its Transportation Secretary, William Coleman, generally regarded Amtrak as an extravagant encumbrance to be given encouragement only sparingly.

However, the Ford administration was persuaded to put a lot of money into a high-speed railroad by a forecast that total inter-city passenger movement in the Corridor would soar from eight million in 1973 to around twenty-seven million by 1990. To redevelop the railway was the

most economical way to cope with the upsurge, as well as the only way to avoid the insufferable environmental damage of still busier airlines and bigger airports, or greater use of automobiles.

The initial objective of the plan is to fit the railway for standard journey times of 2 hours 40 minutes between New York and Washington (226 miles), and 3 hours 40 minutes between New York and Boston (233 miles). The first main task is to make good years of neglected track maintenance, which means virtually re-building 1,000 track-miles of railroad from their foundations. Over fifty curves are to be relaid and realigned for higher speed. No fewer than 770 of the 855 bridges need extensive repair or even, in the case of some 150 built before 1895, complete replacement. Grade crossings are to be eliminated and the whole

route is to be fenced. Fifteen depots in the chief centres of population are to be rebuilt with modern passenger amenities, including escalator access to platforms and capacious automobile parks. A feature of the scheme is electrification throughout on a standard 25kV 60-cycle ac system, which entails replacing all the existing equipment, enlarging tunnels at Baltimore and New York, and a number of bridges elsewhere, to secure the additional clearances essential for overhead wires at this voltage, and electrifying from scratch between New Haven and Boston. At last the nuisance of an electric-diesel traction change-over at New Haven on the New York-Boston run will be eliminated.

Has the North American inter-city passenger train not only been revived as it was dying, but rejuvenated? Is Amtrak

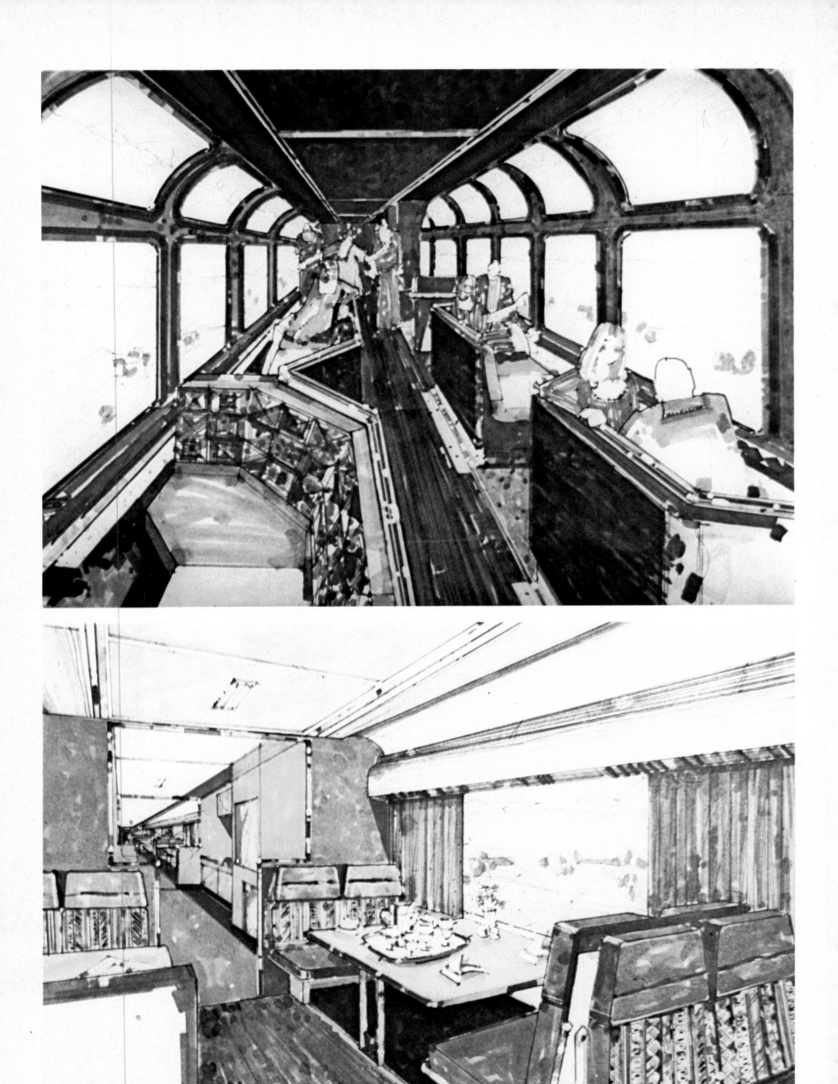

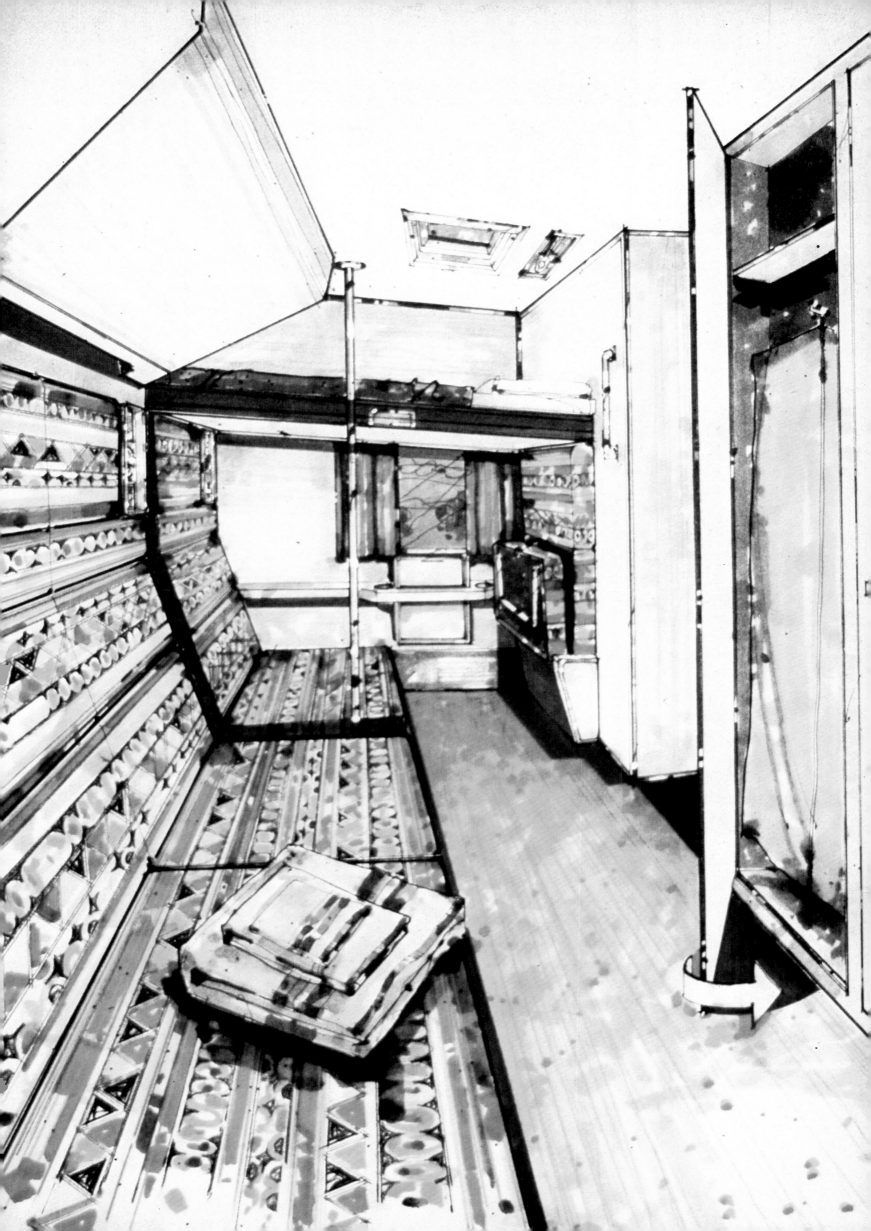

Top: A New York-Washington Metroliner at Philadelphia. *Amtrak*

Above: Amcoach seating seen in close up. *Amtrak*

now heading for the proclaimed objective of its present management — to function efficiently as a profit-centred public corporation, not a spoon-fed Federal agency? Even if it is, the road ahead still looks very long.

Some of Amtrak's thirty-eight routes have recorded encouraging increases of use in the 1970s, particularly where the new Amfleet cars have been commissioned. But in 1977 not one Amtrak scheduled service was showing a margin above its overhead costs. Only a few, like the heavily-patronized New York-Washington Metroliners, the New York-Florida and Chicago-Milwaukee trains and the *Panama* and *Sunset Limiteds*, were covering their direct running expenses. With operating losses already absorbing Federal appropriations of about $1,000,000 a day, and likely to need nearer $2,000,000 by 1980, Amtrak naturally has powerful enemies, not least in Wall Street.

In Washington, at the time of writing the Carter administration has yet fully to declare its hand, though its early enthusiasm for balanced budgeting is ominous for Amtrak. In the first half of the 1970s the combined USA railroads managed an annual investment of no more than $1,400,000,000. Including the redevelopment of the North-East Corridor, Amtrak is seeking to average over $500,000,000 investment annually up to 1981, a figure that may seem disproportionate to both President and Congress when Amtrak's annual output of around thirty million passenger train-miles is set against American railroads' four hundred million or so annual freight train-miles.

The take-over of the North-East Corridor, moreover, injects a new factor into Amtrak's balance sheet. Hitherto, Amtrak has paid its host railroads on an avoidable-cost basis for the use of their tracks, and nothing for railroad maintenance, signalling or traffic control. Arguably, Amtrak has had a bargain and the host — especially in the case of Penn-Central — a large drain on its income. Now the whole bill for running a railroad and all the management-labour problems are laid at Amtrak's door.

Amtrak's outlook was made bleaker by a succession of technical and natural misfortunes that ravaged its services in late 1976 and early 1977. First came repeated derailments of the big SPD40F diesels, which impelled several railroads to apply such crippling speed restrictions to them that hours had to be added to the schedules of trains like the *Empire Builder* and *North Coast Hiawatha*. Research traced the cause to the unsuitability of the SPD40F's six-wheel bogies and suspension to passenger train speed on the indifferently maintained track of many Amtrak routes. That left Amtrak no option but to order a costly rebuilding of the SPD40Fs as lighter, four-wheel bogie machines similar to the subsequent F40PHs from Electromotive.

In addition to that setback, Amtrak had trouble with its passenger equipment. Not unnaturally, with every passing year the ageing long-haul cars it bought from the railroads on its formation became more prone to component defect. To that was added a spate of teething difficulties with its new Amfleet stock, particularly in the braking systems, which at times consigned as much as a fifth to workshops for simultaneous attention. Not that that was all bad, because Amfleet deliveries were running ahead of arrivals of the new diesels with head-end power to feed their electrical auxiliaries!.

Then Pelion was heaped on Ossa by the appalling 1976-77 winter. Quite unable to cope with the phenomenally Arctic conditions, Amtrak had to discontinue temporarily a great many of its services. Derailments, too, were rife. With so much revenue lost, and despite an increase in fares, Amtrak had already fallen $70,000,000 behind its 1977 budget when spring came. Without a vote of emergency funds from Congress it confronted technical bankruptcy and enforced service trimming, even in the highly treasured New York-Washington corridor.

With both the Carter administration and Congress showing hesitation at granting in 1978 even half the funds Amtrak would need to execute its Five-Year Plan on schedule, it looked like the new tomorrow of the North American passenger train could at best be a little late.

RAPID-TRANSIT RAILWAYS ARE IN AGAIN

BY THE 1950s the administrators and planners of North American cities could no longer ignore the peril of unrestricted use of the automobile. The creeping concrete desert that was sterilizing areas of down town Los Angeles was a stark warning of the price to be paid for failure to offer a viable public transport alternative.

Should the money that would be spent go into freeway buses moving smoothly in reserved lanes, or into underground train systems (subways)? There was no doubt that the direct costs of carrying passengers by bus were lower. But city after city corroborated the findings of pioneering research in Toronto: that rail was significantly less expensive when the total costs of setting up a speedy, high-capacity urban transport service by either mode were compared. Toronto reckoned that the extra roadways and fly-overs or dive-unders essential to create room for a free-flowing high-capacity bus service inside the city would cost five times as much as the construction of a new subway. By the early 1960s a number of major North American cities were convinced that they must have new urban rapid-transit railways (some of them, it must be said, without carefully evaluating costs in relation to likely traffic).

The Kennedy administration reacted sympathetically, but Congress stalled the proposals to make Federal money available for new urban transportation development. Not until July 1964 could President Johnson sign the Urban Mass Transportation Act that set the scene for an urban rapid-transit rail revival.

To qualify for the cash grants offered under this Act an authority had to have a fully worked-out urban redevelopment and transportation plan. For transit system improvements required by the plan and approved by the Government, two-thirds of the cost might be Federally funded; the remaining third must be raised locally, and day-to-day running costs would be exclusively a local responsibility.

The subsequent grant rate of around $150,000,000 a year in total was insufficient to cover the big projects several cities had in mind. Moreover, the Federal funds had to be voted annually, which overlaid long-term planning with uncertainty. Eventually, after relentless lobbying by interested parties, Congress and the Nixon administration passed the Urban Mass Transportation

Below: Opening day, 27 March 1976, at Judiciary Square station on the Washington Metro. *WMATA: Phil Portlock*

Assistance Act in late 1970. That provided for more than $1,000,000,000 of Federal money to be ploughed into rapid-transit development in USA cities annually over the following five years, with a promise of continuance at the same rate of support for five years beyond. Cities like Chicago nurturing ambitious programmes to drive new rapid-transit rails down town, could confidently enter into the long-term contracts involved in such large-scale projects.

Chicago, operator of the country's second largest urban rail-transit system, is a city of extremes in this context. The famous loop of double-track railway that gives the city's centre its name is the last old-style elevated railway in the business heart of an American city. Elevated railways survive also in Boston, New York and Philadelphia, but not in the prime downtown area. Yet Chicago showed other US cities the way in integrated planning of new rapid-transit railways and expressways.

The Chicago Transit Authority (CTA) pioneered their idea in 1958 on its Eisenhower route, then applied it extensively to the Dan Ryan extension of 1969. Starting at the elevated system at 18th Street, the Dan Ryan line then occupies the median strip of an expressway all the way from 26th to 95th Street. With the added inducement of stations laid out to simplify transfer from automobile to train, and bus routes redesigned to feed the rail services, the Dan Ryan extension quickly reached a daily flow of more than 100,000 downtown commuters from its nine stations.

Early in 1970 a second extension on the same principle carried the West-Northwest Milwaukee route of the CTA down the middle of the Kennedy Expressway to Jefferson Park. The goal of this projection was the great O'Hare airport, but not until mid-1977 did the Urban Mass Transit Administration (UMTA) in Washington endorse a third grant, of $110,000,000, that will allow the city to complete the downtown-airport direct rail link it has been seeking for a decade.

Chicago would like to be doing much more, but the Federal purse-strings were pulled tightly in the recession of the mid-1970s. As long ago as 1970 the CTA put forward plans for two new downtown subways that would at long last supplant the famous elevated Loop. Even in 1970 the plan was expected to cost $600,000,000, and, although voters in the city areas affected were prepared to pay their share in special taxes, Washington has said that the project is too ambitious for the times.

Cleveland was the first American city to apply rapid-rail transit to the speedy dispersal of a plane-load of passengers in the Jumbo age. In late 1968 it completed an extension to an existing route that now transfers passengers the eleven miles from a terminal beneath Hopkins International Airport's main building to the hub of Cleveland's downtown business district in twenty minutes, including eight intermediate stops. By

highway the trip takes at least twice as long and costs four times as much, even by limousine. Moreover, the Airporter trains, as they are called, run at clockwork ten-minute frequency.

These stainless-steel two-car trainsets, built by Pullman-Standard, are specially styled for airport link traffic. Unlike the usual run of rapid-transit cars, their air-conditioned interiors have spacious floor-to-ceiling luggage racks at each end, and their seating is more roomy. The four 100hp motors on each car give the trains a top speed of 60mph.

The Airporters are governed by an electronic speed and signal control system that is becoming a standard feature of modern rapid rail-transit systems. Command impulses relating to the characteristics of the route and the state of track occupation ahead are fed into the running rails and picked up by underfloor coils mounted on the train

Two views of the Rhode Island Avenue interchange on the Washington Metro. *WMATA: Paul Myatt*

ahead of its leading wheels. On board the train, apparatus translates the impulses into lights on the control cab speedometer which specify the speed at which the train should be moving. Each new command is drawn to the driver's attention by an audible warning; if he does not react appropriately within two and a half seconds, brakes are automatically applied. Most of the commands are automatically originated, but the line's central controller can interpose his own instructions.

Two intermediate stations on the Cleveland Airport extension feature the *sine qua non* of today's rapid transit

Top: A PATH train arriving in Jersey City from New York City. *Port Authority of New York & New Jersey*

Above: A train on Toronto's Yonge Street Subway.

development — ample and easy access for highway riders. Each has a 1,250-auto parking lot, plus well-laid-out space for 'kiss-'n-ride' and 'bus-'n-ride' commuters to enter or leave their vehicles.

The most well-known — or maybe notorious — of North America's rapid-transit systems is unarguably San Francisco's BART (Bay Area Rapid Transit). The idea of an underwater railway to repel the threatened strangulation of the Bay's bridges by swelling highway traffic, was first canvassed in 1946. The State legislature was persuaded that action was vital in face of substantial population growth, and after a co-ordinated develop-

ment and transportation plan for the whole Bay Area had been formulated, a five-county BART District was set up in 1957 with the task of constructing a new rapid-transit rail system. By 1961 it was ready with a plan for the most technically sophisticated and luxurious urban railway the world had seen.

BART District was bidden to finance the scheme by bond issue, serviced by property taxes until maturity in 1999. That made voter approval a pre-requisite, so a mammoth sequence of local community meetings — they ran literally into hundreds — was mounted to sway public opinion. Nevertheless, two of the original five counties were intimidated by the $792,000,000 level of the bond issue. As a result the network plan was reduced to seventy one and a half miles and thirty-four stations in the remaining three counties which, even so, had to carry a bigger share of the finance than they

originally expected. But in November 1962 their voters approved the proposals, albeit by a only slender margin above the percentage level stipulated by the California legislature.

BART's problems started when some dissident taxpayers challenged the legality of the District's constitution and its poll. The six months' delay which that litigation enforced was only a foretaste of what was to come through protracted negotiations leading often to tiresome, time-consuming alteration of design or route. Berkeley's second thoughts that led it to insist on a subway thoughout its city, instead of only part-way, were probably the worst harassment; the argument took two and a half years to resolve and added $18,000,000 to the bill.

When finally, construction could start in June 1964, costs had already risen well above the total estimate of 1962. That had been $996,000,000, taking into account $133,000,000 for the underwater Trans-Bay tube (to be met eventually from Bay Area highway bridge tolls) and a further $71,000,000 for the trains themselves (to be paid for in due course out of operating revenue). It was BART'S further misfortune that its persistently troubled construction ended up in a period when annual inflation ran at a hundred per cent above its analysts' predictions.

There is no doubt that BART was a stupendous project. The remarkable three-and-half mile Trans-Bay tube alone captured exceptional international interest. Six years were occupied with preliminary seismic and soil investigation, followed by detailed design, and four more years in building at a cost of $45,000,000 a mile.

The tube itself, 48ft wide and 24ft high, encases within in its thick, steel-plated concrete shell two rail tunnels and a median duct housing a maintenance walkway and power lines. It was fabricated ashore in fifty-seven 315-350ft sections, each of which was sealed, separately launched into the water ship-fashion, then towed out to be sunk with laser-aided precision in its appointed place as much as 135ft down in a 60ft wide trench that had been dredged in the sea-bed. The welding together of the sections underwater had to leave the tube flexible. Each joint allows two to four inches of free play upwards, sideways or lengthways, and the whole tube has some freedom of integral lateral and vertical movement — a vital precaution in this earthquake-sensitive area. Thousands of Bay Area folk enthusiastically took the opportunity to walk or cycle through the tube after its completion and before it was closed to allow tracklaying to begin.

The BART network is roughly X-shaped, with the Trans-Bay tube beginning the lower left arm that leads from the Oakland City Center-12th Street interchange to San Francisco and the West Bay. Only twenty-seven miles of the entire system are laid at ground level; twenty-five miles are elevated and nineteen (in addition to the Trans-Bay tube) underground. Much of the subway construction was as taxing as the work on the Trans-Bay tube, particularly the stretch under San Francisco's Market Street, where the city's streetcars were put underground at the same time and complex grade-separated junctions and matching five-level stations had to be excavated amid a maze of civic utility mains, power lines and pipes.

Above ground the BART system, like Chicago's, exploits the advantages of using the median strip of new highways in several areas (the twenty-two BART stations with parking lots have room for almost 17,700 automobiles). Determined that the railway should be an aesthetic pride as well as a respected service in the Bay Area, BART empanelled sixteen architectural and eight landscaping concerns to shape the well-equipped stations. Many of them have gained awards for their originality in the use of concrete and steel, glass and quarry tiles, and for their mosaics, fountains and other landscaping features.

The railway was planned as a new technological wonder of the world. For a start, claiming that it was proven to make for optimum stability and smoothness of ride, BART chose a 5ft 6in track gauge – 9½in wider than any other North American rail system. The third-rail electrification method selected was not unusual, but by previous standards the voltage of 1,000 was high for this arrangement. Instead of following custom and leaving vehicle design largely to experienced professionals, BART engineers not only designed their own cars but gave the contract to an aerospace concern, Rohr, which was just breaking into the railroad car-building market.

The aluminium-bodied, air-conditioned cars ride on air-cushion springs and are pleasantly carpeted and furnished within. Every car, with or without driving controls, has four 150mph traction motors, one per axle, to enable a train to achieve the originally planned average speed of 42mph, stops included, and sustain 80mph between stops. A train can accelerate at 3mph per second – and decelerate at the same pace, using its dynamic brakes down to around 4mph and tread brakes for the final slowing to a stop.

The whole railway was designed for automatic operation from a single computerized control centre. Not only the trains' starts and stops, but also the opening and closing of their doors at stops, and their running from second to second, were to be remotely controlled. Comparing performance with its memorized timetable, the computer would accelerate or decelerate trains as necessary to observe schedule; in the event of a bad failure, it would instantaneously present the despatchers in the control centre with the best temporary revision of the timetable to sort out the trouble as

quickly as possible. At stations, approaching trains would announce themselves by transmitting a coded signal to activate the eight computer-operated electronic train destination and information displays mounted on each platform.

Fare collection and control, too, was wholly automated. There were change-giving and ticket machines, able to accept $1 or $5 bills, to sell either single-ride or stored-ride tickets adding up to $20 in value. A partially-used stored-ride ticket could be returned to the machine for appropriate credit against a new one. Turnstile machines endorsed the ticket with time, date and station, retaining a single-ride ticket but returning a stored-ride ticket with the remaining cash balance calculated and printed on it for the passenger's guidance. An invalid ticket, needless to say, would be rejected and the turnstile automatically held

closed against the offender, who would have to put money in another, 'adfare' machine to get the appropriate added value printed on the ticket for acceptance by the turnstile.

Long before any of the BART system was ready for traffic the project ran into serious financial trouble. During 1966 it was clear there would be a shortfall of around $150,000,000 on the inflated construction costs. BART management stubbornly refused to trim the network and eventually, in the spring of 1969, the California State legislature agreed to a further issue of bonds, to be serviced from a sales tax in BART territory. Soon, there came the relief of the UMTA Act, which made Federal grants available and even allowed some elaboration of the original plans. The $160,000,000 cost of the 450-car BART fleet, too, was sixty-four per cent covered by Federal money.

Right: A rubber-tyred train-set of the Montreal Metro. *Montreal Urban Community Transit Commission*

However, only $315,000,000 of BART's $1,600,000,000 final bill came from Federal funds, because the project had been launched so far in advance of the UMTA Act.

BART's troubles were not over when the line was ready for use. The great technological leap forward had been a foot or two too far. BART's enormously complex computerized control system was not foolproof — as was vividly demonstrated by an incident when a train approaching the dead-end Fremont terminus received and acted upon a full-speed acceleration command instead of slow-down order. Consequently State safety inspectors would not agree to operation through the Trans-Bay tube with the existing safety and control systems, for the timetable was based on funnelling 80mph trains from the converging routes through the tunnel at just two-minute headway, and a back-up lineside signalling system had to be hastily installed.

Eventually, on 16 September 1974, the Trans-Bay tube was opened to passenger-carrying service. Up to the time of writing BART has still to perfect the reliability of its equipment so that it can run a service of the intensity originally planned, instead of at a minimum five-minute headway, and realize its full ridership potential.

That an up-to-date rapid-transit railway can persuade commuters to leave their automobiles is demonstrated by the fourteen-and-a-half-mile line of PATCO (Port Authority Transit Corporation, a subsidiary of the Delaware River Port Authority which runs from down town Philadelphia to the dormitory area of Lindenwold, New Jersey. Created in 1969 by linking an existing subway with the nearly two-miles long Benjamin Franklin bridge over the Delaware and the right of way of a former railroad line, the PATCO system has almost doubled the six million riders a year with which it began.

Interestingly, the seventy-five Budd-built cars of the PATCO fleet embody a lot of the automatic control devices used by BART, but PATCO has had little trouble. As on BART, a train's motorman is there primarily as insurance. He can take over control of the train in an emergency, has continuous radio contact with a dispatcher, and can talk to passengers over the public address system; but otherwise he has only to monitor the dials on his control console as the Automatic Control System (ATC) starts, runs and stops his train, and opens and closes its doors. In addition to automatic fare dispensing and checking equipment, the fourteen stations have closed-circuit television surveillance.

PATCO is divorced from the Southeastern Pennsylvania Transportation Authority (SEPTA), which exemplifies another facet of the North American public transport revival — the formation of regional authorities to co-ordinate all systems in major urban areas. Founded in 1963, SEPTA represents five counties and, with powers to own and operate as well as lease, has the entire commuter rail system of the region, and Philadelphia's rapid-transit bus lines, under contract. Likewise, the Massachussetts Bay Transportation Authority (MBTA) integrates the railroad commuter, rapid-transit rail, streetcar and bus systems throughout an area populated by two and a half million and covering nearly eighty cities, towns and other communities surrounding Boston.

Well over half of all rapid-rail transit operation in the USA centres on New York, which started its famous network of elevated railways in the 1870s. The elevated system is now reduced to a few stretches in outlying districts, for the city started to bury its lines underground in 1904.

Today's New York subway system was developed in two major expansions, one just before and the other shortly after the Second World War. The three divisions of the 246-mile network, which runs over 5,500 cars and moves over a million passengers annually from its 462 stations, originally comprised two privately-owned and one public company, but in 1940 the entire network was brought under the city's control. Since 1953 the powers have been exercised by the New York City Transit Authority, under the jurisdiction of the New York State's Metropolitan Transportation Authority since early 1968.

New York is at work on fresh subway extensions, among them a new four-track tunnel under the East River, but was pressed for cash in the mid-1970s, as all the world knows. Consequently its most ambitious project, a new north-south line beneath Manhattan's Second Avenue — which would drive a sixth route across the island — had to be shelved in 1975

after three years' work, and is unlikely to be started again until the 1980s.

The New York Subway is not renowned for the modernity of its vehicles. Flying in the face of forward-looking design that is to be found almost everywhere else, it still goes for conventional heavyweights; a non-air-conditioned New York car weighs almost half as much again as Boston's latest air-conditioned vehicle. However, New Yorkers can get the measure of up-to-date, aluminium-bodied, air-conditioned car design on the nearby PATH line from the 'Big Apple' to Newark.

In 1962 the States of New York and New Jersey co-operated to establish the Port Authority Trans-Hudson Authority (PATH) and salvage a destitute railroad that ran uncertainly from Manhattan through the Hudson River tubes to Hoboken and Newark (over Pennsylvania tracks for completion of the Newark run). Since 1962 PATH has spent over $250,000,000 to revitalize and re-equip the line, converting it to a prime specimen of modern rapid-transit.

Besides its original 33rd Street terminal in New York, PATH has since 1971 operated from a brand-new terminal beneath the towering World Trade Center in lower Manhattan; and in 1975 it completed a proud new Transportation Center in New Jersey. PATH is anxious to extend right into Newark airport and also to gain access to New York's Penn station as soon as it qualifies for UMTA assistance. Its aim, amongst other things, is to set up a direct rail link from Manhattan to Kennedy Airport, using Long Island Railroad tracks en route.

A North American subway with a type of track and wheels unique of the Rio Grande (down south, neighbouring Mexico City has adopted the same system) is Montreal, which adopted the rubber-tyre system perfected by RATP, the Paris transport authority, for the Paris Metro in the 1950s. The Montreal cars have steel wheels and below them orthodox steel rails; but the wheels do not touch the rails unless there is an emergency. The main carrying wheels are mounted outside the steel wheels and are rubber-tyred. The rubber-tyred running wheels rest on flat concrete runways, which are the principal element of the track; but because they are flat they cannot guide round curves, so each bogie is also fitted both sides with horizontally mounted, rubber-tyred guide wheels that ride against continuous flat rails laid sideways-on to the train, at a fixed gauge, just above the level of the running rails. Only in the event of tyre failure should the steel wheels come into

Top and centre: Two views of Finch station, terminus of Toronto's Yonge Street Subway, showing the spacious provision for transfer from automobile to train.

Bottom: Pentagon station on the Washington Metro. *WMATA: Paul Myatt*

contact with the rails.

The chief advantage of the rubber-tyre system is its greatly enhanced adhesion in the always dry environment of a subway (the benefit is totally nullified in the open, of course). That means time saving through smarter acceleration to top speed; smooth deceleration can be achieved more quickly, too. The advantages can be vividly seen on sections of the Paris Metro, where the line is sharply dipped between many stations — a touch of power, and a rubber-tyred train is up to top speed before it is clear of the platform; then at the next stop braking of the momentum can be left until the head of the train is in the station.

The rubber-tyre concept has it flaws, the chief being the excessive heat generated by the friction of tyres and runways. Both Paris and Montreal have had serious trouble on this count. Another disadvantage is that exceptional acceleration and deceleration call for considerable power; the energy consumption of rubber-tyred systems, therefore, tends to be higher than that of conventional rapid-transit railways.

North America's newest rapid-transit venture at the time of writing is the Washington Metro, which, after running into nearly as much political tribulation as BART, finally opened its first section of four and a half miles in March 1976. A comprehensively automated system, the Washington Metro is planned eventually to run to ninety-eight route-miles serving fifty-three air-conditioned subway stations down town and thirty-four on the surface in the suburbs — all for a total bill of at least $4,500,000,000, of which over $1,500,000,000 had been advanced from Federal funds by the end of 1976. If cash flows satisfactorily, the whole network could be active by the end of 1983. Next to follow Washington will be Atlanta, where the first stage of a fifty-mile network is due to open at the end 1978. Baltimore has begun building; and Miami hopes to start construction by 1979.

Whether Miami or any more American cities will be able to embark on new full-scale rapid-transit rail systems on the traditional pattern is now extremely doubtful. By the spring of 1977 the operating costs of the new networks, apart from the expense of construction, were frightening Washington. President Carter was prompted to protest to his Transportation Secretary that many of the rapid-transit systems were being 'grossly overdesigned'. It was time, he suggested, to dismiss the tunnellers and look again at surface rail operation. Moreover, although the annual rate of Federal grant had by 1977 soared to $2,000,000,000 (and had been resolutely pegged at that level), the scale of systems being planned, and inflation in costs, meant that there was going to be nowhere near enough capital for every aspiring rapid-rail transit city from Federal funds.

For cities like Buffalo, Dayton, Denver, Detroit and Pittsburgh, the rapid-transit future may lie with Light Rapid Transit and Light Rail Vehicles. Essentially these two combine as modernization of the old-style trolley car system now being extensively exploited on the mainland of Western Europe. Advocates of LRT and LRV tirelessly proclaim that their system is far cheaper to build than conventional rapid-rail transit, and that it is much less expensive to operate than buses. The latter argument derives partly from the impressive passenger capacity of the modern LRV. The articulated 75ft-long twin-car which Boeing-Vertol, the helicopter division of the aerospace firm, is currently supplying to Boston and San Francisco as replacements of old street-cars, for example, can seat sixty-eight passengers for an inclusive weight of around thirty tons. Something like this could be North America's tracked rapid-transit train of tomorrow.

Below: The impressive Journal Square Transportation Centre interchange of the PATH system in Jersey City. Port Authority of New York & New Jersey

RAILROAD INDENTIFICATION GUIDE

Union Pacific Centennial diesel-electric
locomotive Class DDA 40X of 6,600hp.

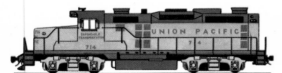

Class GP20 general-purpose 2,000hp
diesel-electric switcher.

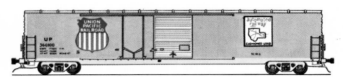

UP standard boxcars range from 50ft to 86ft
in length and have hydraulically
cushioned underframes.

UP Pullman as used in remaining
long-distance passenger services.

Open gondala wagon for 70-ton loads.

TOFC wagon of 65 short tons capacity
and two refrigerated semi-trailers of
joint SP-Union Pacific fruit transport
company.

High-capacity boxcar with cushioned
suspension for delicate loads.

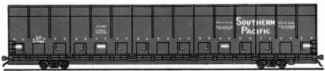

Vert-a-Pac boxcar designed to carry
partly assembled motorcars stacked
vertically inside.

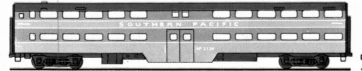

Double-deck passenger car for
commuter services in the San Francisco
area.

Clifford & Wendy Meadway

EMD 3,600hp SD45T-2 diesel-electric
freight locomotive.

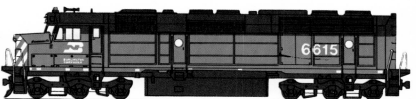

Class F45 EMD 3,600hp diesel-electric locomotive with GM 20-cylinder engine.

A full dome car used on BN top passenger services.

Class E8A EMD 2,250hp diesel-electric locomotive used on Chicago commuter service.

Class SW1500 EMD 1,500hp diesel-electric shunter.

100-ton coal hopper of 1970 delivery.

Clifford & Wendy Meadway

Logo of the Atchison, Topeka & Santa Fe Railway Company.

A container and a road semi-trailer on a flat wagon designed for piggyback traffic.

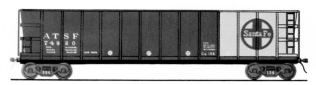

3,600hp diesel-electric locomotive as used on 84-wagon coal trains.

Solid-bottom gondola car of the type used on the 84-unit block coal trains.

Refrigerator wagon with mechanical temperature control and shock-absorbing underframe.

An EMD F45 diesel-electric locomotive in earlier Santa Fe passenger colours, now being repainted in the blue/yellow livery seen above.

Clifford & Wendy Meadway

Illinois Central Railroad

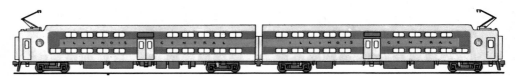

Double-deck electric two-car trainset
for IC suburban services.

Trailer Train flatcar with two piggyback
road trailers.

EMD GP40 3,000hp diesel-electric
locomotive.

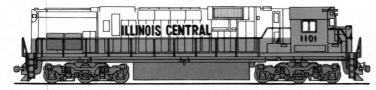

Alco C636 3,600hp diesel-electric
locomotive

Boxcar with 50ft internal length and
110,000lb capacity.

Clifford & Wendy Meadway

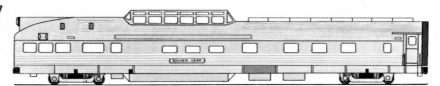

Denver & Rio Grande Western Railroad
dome car for Zephyr trains.

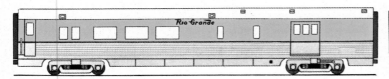

Baggage/crew car and diesel-electric locomotive for Zephyr trains.

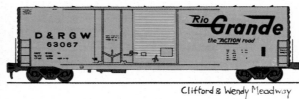

Class DE CC98 (EMD SD45) 3,600hp freight
locomotive.

Bogie boxcar of 75-ton load capacity.

Clifford & Wendy Meadway

Special 85ft coach with driving end for GO (Ontario) commuter trains, operated by Canadian National Railways.

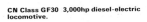

Modern Canadian National stainless-steel passenger coach of Budd design with disc brakes.

CN Class GPA17 1,750hp diesel-electric locomotive.

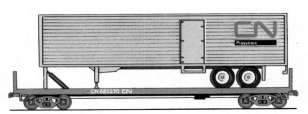

CN Class GF30 3,000hp diesel-electric locomotive.

CN bogie flat wagon designed to take piggyback road semi-trailers up to 39ft 7in long.

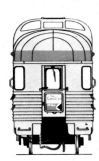

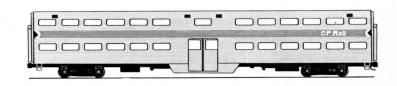

Profile of the lounge car shown at bottom left.

A 168-seat double-deck coach of a new commuter train introduced in 1970 by Canadian Pacific on its Montreal-Lake Shore service.

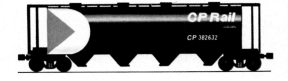

A 2400hp Bo-Bo diesel-electric locomotive of CP Rail Class DRF 24C built by M L Worthington in 1966.

A CP Rail 100-ton bottom-discharge covered hopper wagon.

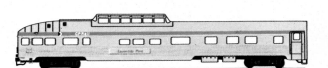

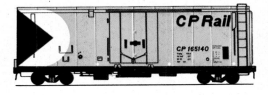

A CP Rail Park-class lounge car used in inter-city expresses such as the trans-continental Canadian.

Standard insulated box car.

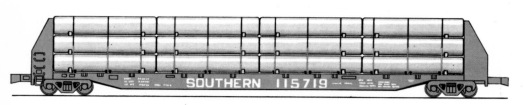

US Southern Railway 100-ton bogie flat specially built for concrete pipe transport.

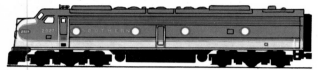

EMD E8 2,250hp diesel-electric passenger locomotive.

Pullman car for streamlined passenger trains.

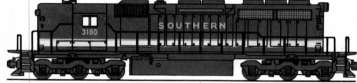

SD40 3,000hp diesel-electric freight locomotive.

SR standard bogie box car.

Clifford & Wendy Meadway

Louisville & Nashville Railroad Company's saddleback flat wagon for heavy road vehicle haulage.

L & N EMD GP30 2,250hp diesel-electric freight locomotive.

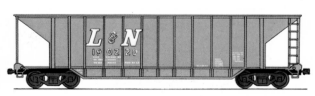

L & N-designed and built 100-ton quick-dump coal hopper for merry-go-round working.

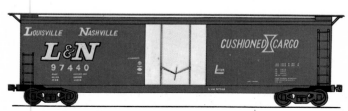

L & N 70-ton boxcar for high-value freight.

Clifford & Wendy Meadway

Standard caboose built in L & N shops from 1963 to 1971.